THE EDUCATION OF CHILDREN
WHO ARE LOOKED-AFTER

pbell

N.

967

nfer

INVESTOR IN PEOPLE

DEDICATION

This report is dedicated to the memory of Tory Laughlan (1944-1994) the founder-director of *The Who Cares? Trust*. Tory's immense charm and gentleness, vision and wisdom, complemented a relentless determination to strive for the very best for young people looked-after and an abiding faith in the very best that was in them.

Published in March 1997
by the National Foundation for Educational Research,
The Mere, Upton Park, Slough, Berkshire SL1 2DQ

CONTENTS

Ackowledgements   i

CHAPTER 1: INTRODUCTION   1
  Background   1
  Salient recent initiatives   3
  The present report   6
  Who are 'Children who are Looked-After'?   7
  Connections with special education   15
  Outline of report   16

CHAPTER 2: THE NATIONAL POSITION   17
  The questionnaire responses   17
  Provision for the education of looked-after children   19
  Organisational problems   22
  Positive initiatives – some examples   25
  Policy documents   30
  Monitoring and evaluation   33
  Small-scale research/data collection exercises   33
  Pilot studies   34
  Conclusions   37
  Summary   38

**CHAPTER 3: THE SOCIAL SERVICES' EDUCATION
SUPPORT SERVICES – STAFF, USERS, AIMS & PRINCIPLES**   40
  The organisation and management of the services   40
  Initiation of the services   41
  The staff   43
  The service briefs   44
  Users of the services   46
  The characteristics of the young people   50
  The fundamental issues to be addressed   54
  Summary   55

**CHAPTER 4: THE EDUCATION SUPPORT SERVICES
– PRACTICE**   58
  Mediation   58
  Informing   60
  Meetings and reviews   66
  Managing information   66
  Case loads   68
  Induction programmes   68
  Task-related support   70
  Arranging packages   72
  Individual Education Plans   72
  Other supportive initiatives   73
  Some case examples   74
  Praise and reward   76

Training   79
After care? Post 16 careers   81
Summary   84

CHAPTER 5: THE CARERS   86
Introduction   86
The carers involved in the research   86
The young people for whom they cared   90
The practical impact of education on care placements   92
Foster carers' intervention in the education of the children
  they looked after   96
Residential carers' intervention in the education of
  young people they cared for   99
Factors militating against education stability in residential care   105
Transforming residential homes   105
Summary   107

CHAPTER 6: THE SCHOOLS   110
Schools' attitudes to pupils who are looked-after   111
Admissions   112
Exclusions   119
Maintenance   128
Alternative education provision   131
Initiatives in school clusters   132
A case study of the consequences of 'failure'   133
'Successes'   136
Summary   137

**CHAPTER 7: GENERAL ISSUES, CONCLUSIONS &
        RECOMMENDATIONS**   140
Resources   140
The criteria for success   145
The environment of the social services and education departments   146
The future of the services   148

RECOMMENDATIONS   151
  Commonality   152
  Audit of provision   152
  Awareness of consequences   153
  Flexibility and speed of response   153
  Professional boundaries   154
  Nature of support   154
  Partnership   154
  Carers   155
  Data   155
  Service management posts   155
  Support of service management   156

REFERENCES   157

ACKNOWLEDGEMENTS

I should like to thank the many colleagues at the NFER who have contributed to the production of this report, in particular, Anne Wilkin, Alison Wakefield and Michael Ridout for invaluable assistance with the interview programme; the project advisory group, representing social services and education practitioners, inspectors, directors and service managers; and carers, officers in local authorities, teachers, support service staff and young people for giving up valuable time in order to talk with members of the research team.

CHAPTER 1
INTRODUCTION

Background

Research into the Education of Children in Care was first undertaken at the National Foundation for Educational Research (NFER) in 1988/89 following Sonia Jackson's (1987) seminal identification of the lack of work in this area; the resultant report (Fletcher-Campbell and Hall, 1990) was able to give a thorough delineation of the problems and establish what needed to be done but, from lack of empirical evidence available at the time, was unable to describe mature, systematic good practice established throughout a local authority. It has thus been extremely encouraging to return to the research area a few years later and find a burgeoning of relevant and maturing good practice and be able to report in this present volume on initiatives that have proved, and are proving, themselves effective.

The intervening years between the two research projects have seen rapid change in both social services and education legislation and policy-making, all of which has impinged on the focus of the research. Indeed, perhaps the most critical finding of the most recent research, reinforcing but developing findings from the earlier NFER project, was that the extreme vulnerability of young people who are looked-after means that they are disproportionately disadvantaged by any 'roughness' or deficiencies in the education or welfare systems and are at the centre of a clutch of disadvantages emerging within the present political and social climate. Very broadly, these young people are growing up amongst social disorder and rising crime rates, substance abuse, unemployment, domestic breakdown and child abuse. More particularly, within education, Local Management of Schools, the publication of school performance in national assessment, the changing nature of the Local Education Authority, and innovations such as Pupil Referral Units are all relevant, as is the later legislation within the Education Act 1993 and associated *Code of Practice* (DFE, 1994), school exclusion and truancy, the reorganisation of special education provision and support, resource allocation within education, institutional pressures such as rises in class size and inter-institutional competition.

Within social services, the Children Act 1989 has, of course, had a considerable impact (not least by redefining 'in care' and introducing a new concept of 'in need') together with reorganisation following the official reports on residential care and the structure of the social work profession. Overall financial stringency and a greater awareness of the need for accountability throughout local authorities have also had an impact on all policy and practice.

These changes in both Education and Social Services departments are not tangential to the educational experiences and careers of children who are looked-after. These children, paradigmatically, are surrounded by support and welfare services and professionals. Intervening in the life of any one child who is looked-after may be LEA officers, educational psychologists, child psychiatrists, special educational needs support service staff (particularly in relation to emotional and behavioural difficulties), education welfare officers, therapists, field and residential social workers, review managers, foster carers and youth justice workers – all in addition to the usual set of professionals with whom any child will have contact (teachers, general practitioners, counsellors). Furthermore, their families may be involved with rent and debt collectors or the police – all making, as one social worker commented, 'a steady stream of professionals walking up their front path'. There can, at times, be so many people involved with a child or a family that the individual or the family becomes submerged (this was an issue raised with regard to reviews, as discussed later). The upshot of this is that any systemic changes, however slight, in any professional practice will have the potential to affect the life of the child or the family; if anyone is buffeted in the slipstreams of life, these young people will be. That a butterfly in the western hemisphere can 'cause' a hurricane in the eastern hemisphere is now a well-worn cliché within explanations of chaos theory: but the conceit can be accurately applied to the lives of many children who are looked-after. What may appear minor changes taken by themselves or applied to other situations may further disrupt lives already characterised by instability and fragmentation.

It is, thus, important to remember that young people who come into the care system in whatever way and for whatever reason, may not be in a position to make 'normal' responses. The implications of this will be discussed later in this report – for there is cogent evidence to justify positive discrimination and discrete support. Yet, concomitantly, as one foster carer said: 'Why should their education be any different from that of other children just because they are in care?'. A strong perception running through all those committed to discrete support for the education of young people who are looked-after was that it was merely in place to ensure entitlement and to restore what in other circumstances would accrue to the young person 'normally'. What is 'normally available' is, very often, not thus available to children and young people who are looked-after, by virtue of that very same legal 'status' and involvement in the care system which, inevitably, brings with it fragmentation and a disjunction from the 'normality' which so much of life assumes. Those involved in the provision of effective education to the young people concerned are increasingly aware that their role consists in repairing the effects of that fragmentation and using education placements and plans to *complement* – and often, *fulfil* – care placements and plans. This theme, quintessentially to do with concepts of 'integration' and 'inclusion', will underpin much of the substance of the data that follow in this report.

Salient recent initiatives

In the years between the two NFER reports there have been significant developments directly relating to the education of children who are looked-after. These are briefly summarised below.

Documentation

Both the Utting Report (1991) and the Warner Report (1992) identified the importance of attending to education for children with whom social services were involved. More importantly, though less obviously, the reports challenged practice in residential care; the significance of this in relation to young people's education will be discussed later in this report. There was research evidence, for example, that the overall management of residential units was a critical factor to the nurturing of education within those units; education was not a bolt-on extra – it was something that had to be integrated into the whole *modus vivendi*.

The Audit Commission (1994), in the course of investigating the co-ordination of community child health and social services for children in need, identified the lack of attention to education issues in the authorities which they visited and commented on the way in which colleagues cast the blame on each other: social services staff criticised education departments for not providing sufficient alternative education, while education officers criticised their social services colleagues for not intervening early enough to prevent difficulties arising with school placements. The commissioners commented that 'meanwhile children missed their education' (para 95) but did not suggest that there might be a relationship between the stability of care and school placements – understandably, perhaps, considering that they had not investigated educational issues in depth.

A joint circular from the Department of Health and the Department for Education (GB. DFE, 1994) issued guidance regarding the role of schools and carers, and stressed the importance of inter-agency collaboration to ensure that the education of children looked-after was effectively managed. The circular was unequivocal in underlining that 'wherever children looked after are placed, their education should always be a prime consideration and the various authorities involved should always co-operate to see that effective educational provision is made' (p20, para 52).

The joint report by the Office for Standards in Education (Ofsted) and the Social Services Inspectorate (SSI) (1995) was more focused, hard-hittingly providing empirical evidence of poor educational achievement, the low priority given to education by professionals working with children who were looked-after, poor liaison between professionals and a lack of co-ordination between services, inadequate communication and management of information, lethargy in decision-making and negligible specific training for relevant professionals. The inspectors' final recommendation was: 'As a matter of urgency SSD, LEAs and schools need to work together to devise ways of ensuring an appropriate educational placement and entitlement for these children' (p44, para 92).

The development of existing services

A few authorities had established discrete services around 1990, prior to the recommendations and guidance given in the documentation described above. In the main, these services, representing a considerable number of teachers, had evolved as a result of the redeployment of staff following the closure of Community Homes with Education or education units on the site of residential children's homes. The reasons for these closures are various and, perhaps, not entirely relevant here. The position was not unaffected by the advent of the National Curriculum, intended to provide a broad, balanced curriculum for all young people of statutory school age (although social services education units were not legally bound to offer the National Curriculum); parallel developments within special education, which moved from the idea of segregated provision towards that of including pupils in mainstream provision; and parallel developments within Health, where there was increasing awareness of the necessity to keep people with needs within their own communities. Furthermore, many authorities were seeking to rationalise their care provision and were looking for economies in the light of financial stringency. However, although these closures seemed to be a catalyst for innovative services in those few authorities which were at the forefront of establishing specialist education support services, there have since been openings elsewhere. One authority, for example, despite an ostensible interest in the possibilities afforded by maintaining young people looked-after within mainstream schools in their own communities, has chosen to open a new Community Home with Education, going against trends elsewhere.

Practice in the 'early' authorities has developed and matured and has informed the present research; indeed, the 'maturity' of the provision was one of the criteria for selection of authorities for case study work in the NFER project (see below) on the grounds that it was here that most could be learnt, in that problems had been thought about and worked through. However, it ought to be pointed out at this stage that the forerunners, enjoying a significant staffing establishment, themselves admitted that it was unlikely that their services would be established in 1996 as they had been five or six years – or whenever – previously. Changing political contexts, expectations of providers and financial situations mean that few authorities can, as they approach the millennium, countenance establishing services on the scale, *per capita*, that some of the early services represent. The present report will bear the realities of this in mind as it discusses practice even though, without exception, all those who had had contact with the specialist services in the case study authorities visited as part of the NFER research, articulated their chief 'complaint' about the service as being that 'there is not enough of it'.

Other activity

The awareness raising represented by the documentation referred to above was reinforced by national conferences (organised by, for example, Ofsted and SSI to disseminate the findings of the inspection report) and voluntary organisations (the Royal Philanthropic Society and the Who Cares? Trust); conferences organised by local authorities both for their own staff and, sometimes, for colleagues from other authorities; and media coverage (see, for example, Holdsworth, 1995; McParlin, 1995; Meegan, 1996). Both the Who Cares? Trust and the National Children's Bureau developed initiatives, the former by the appointment of a full-time education development manager with a national brief, the latter by specific projects, working in particular areas. The issue of the education of children looked-after has increasingly come under scrutiny by researchers both in its own right (Aldgate *et al.*, 1993) and within projects principally focused on other issues in either education or care (see, for example, Blyth and Milner, 1994; Stein, 1994; Biehal *et al.*, 1995; Triseliotis *et al.*, 1995; Action on Aftercare Consortium, 1996.). An informal national network of committed and experienced practitioners began to be established and it was apparent that these people were, albeit often in different ways, addressing the problems and finding that many of them were not intractable, given awareness and commitment allied to sound management.

The present report

The present report describes what was happening as regards the education of children looked-after in 1996. It represents data gathered during a twelve-month research project within the NFER's Membership Programme, sponsored by the Council of Local Education Authorities (CLEA).

The *aims* of the project were:

♦ to delineate any changes in policy, procedures and practice that had come about, or were in the process of being implemented, as a result of LEAs' responses to the DFE Circular;

♦ to explore the resource, managerial and training implications of these changes at the level of the local authority;

♦ to describe the perceived effects on the young people concerned, particularly with regard to their educational experiences and careers, and motivation and achievement at school;

♦ to establish criteria for good practice within a context in which the interaction of social and educational needs is critical;

♦ to identify the implications for local authorities and for those schools which have looked-after children on their roll.

Methodology
Phase 1
A questionnaire was sent to all local authorities in England and Wales seeking information about their present and planned provision to support the education of children looked-after. Respondents were invited to return any relevant documentation. At the same time, initial exploratory interviews were conducted in 14 local authorities which were known to the research team as having initiated specialist provision or which were in the process of so doing.

Phase 2
Case studies were conducted in six local authorities identified from phase 1 as having interesting, fairly well developed practice by way of a discrete education support service for children looked-after; of these, three were metropolitan boroughs and three shire counties. The interview programme in these authorities varied according to structures (for example, the organisation of social work teams and geographical considerations) and

relevant contextual variables (such as the effect of imminent local government reform or the socio-economic nature of administrative districts). In each, a range of staff was interviewed, including area, team and unit managers, foster carers, youth justice workers and education support service staff within social services; and head teachers, class teachers, project workers and officers within education. Where appropriate, researchers spoke with young people who had experienced intervention from the education support service, relevant meetings were attended and documentation was collected.

Telephone interviews were conducted in a further 13 authorities in order to follow-up their questionnaire responses.

Who are 'Children who are Looked-After'?

The Children Act 1989 introduced new terminology for children previously known as being 'in care'. The broad term 'looked-after' (see section 22(1) of the Act) embraces all those young people for whom the local authority has some degree of formal responsibility. The broad term includes children who are 'accommodated' – where the local authority shares responsibility with the child's birth parents and substitute parents (this used to be known as 'voluntary care'); and those 'in care' – when they are subject to a court order under section 31(1)(a), or an interim order under section 38, of the Children Act 1989. The latter would usually be the case if they had been subject to severe physical, emotional or sexual abuse or neglect. The differences are not merely pedantic or merely having legal significance – the research showed that they could affect a young person's educational experience. If 'accommodated', for example, there could be excessive disruption as birth parents fluctuated in their decisions as to whether their child was or was not to be looked-after at any one time. If 'in care', it was often necessary to move a child from his or her existing school place so that the parents from whom the child had been removed for whatever reason did not interfere in his or her new life – for example, by turning up at the school gates at the end of the school session. These issues will be discussed in later chapters.

Government statistics show that at 31 March 1994, the most recent year for which figures are available, there was a total of 49,000 young people in care. Table 1.1 shows proportions looked-after in the case study authorities.

Table 1.1   Number of looked-after children of statutory school age* as at 31 March 1994: percentage of children aged under 18

	% **
All England	0.4
Case study authority A	0.3
Case study authority B	0.5
Case study authority C	0.8
Case study authority D	0.4
Case study authority E	0.3
Case study authority F	0.5

*   on account of the way in which DoH statistics are presented, the total of statutory school age includes young people who are 17.

** figures are rounded to the nearest decimal point

(*source: Department of Health, 1996b*)

Table 1.2 shows distribution by age (figures for early years and for young people above statutory school age have been omitted).

Table 1.2   Age distribution of looked-after children of statutory school age as at 31 March 1994: percentages of total school aged population looked-after

	aged 5-9	aged 10-15	aged 16-17
All England	24	52	24
Case study authority A	24	53	23
Case study authority B	32	51	17
Case study authority C	31	49	20
Case study authority D	25	55	21
Case study authority E	18	56	26
Case study authority F	20	53	27

(*source: Department of Health, 1996b*)

It will be noted that the way in which the Department of Health collects data is not readily useful for considering education. Department for Education and Employment statistics categorise according to phase of schooling (primary – secondary) for example, and use the age of 16 – the end of statutory schooling – as a category limit.

Most of the specialist education support for young people looked-after is directed towards adolescents; this is reasonable in the light of the age distribution shown in table 1.2, although the issue of the age range with which specialist services worked will be discussed in chapter three.

It should be pointed out that the overall numbers in care represent a 'snapshot': the 'flux' – the movement in and out of looked-after status – is considerable in some areas (see table 1.3) and the duration in care is various (table 1.4).

Table 1.3 **Flux in looked-after population: total cases started and ceased to be looked-after in the year ending 31 March 1994 as percentage of total looked-after on 31 March 1994.**

	cases
All England	128 %
Case study authority A	143 %
Case study authority B	87 %
Case study authority C	138 %
Case study authority D	106 %
Case study authority E	108 %
Case study authority F	103 %

(source: Department of Health, 1996b)

Table 1.4 **All children looked after at 31 March 1994: percentages by duration of being looked-after**

	< 6 mths	6 mths - 2 yrs	2 - 5 yrs	> 5 yrs
All England	18	27	31	23
Case study authority A	27	34	25	25
Case study authority B	16	26	33	24
Case study authority C	16	43	29	25
Case study authority D	15	24	34	17
Case study authority E	18	20	26	36
Case study authority F	15	28	32	24

(total may not sum to 100 because of rounding)

(source: Department of Health, 1996b)

Some young people spend many years permanently in care while others experience only a short episode. This fluctuating population poses a significant management problem to those providing specialist educational services to these young people, as will be discussed in chapter 3. Table 1.5 shows the patterns of where the young people live.

Table 1.5 All children looked-after at 31 March 1994: placements as percentage of total looked-after

	foster home	residential home	with parents	other *
All England	62	15	9	12
Case study authority A	50	25	15	10
Case study authority B	54	18	16	11
Case study authority C	67	8	11	14
Case study authority D	69	10	10	12
Case study authority E	63	17	5	14
Case study authority F	65	10	13	13

total may not sum to 100 because of rounding
* includes placement for adoption and lodgings/independent living

(*source: Department of Health, 1996b*)

In terms of the actual numbers involved it might seem that foster placements should attract the most support. However, as will be seen later, most authorities considered that the most entrenched problems and the children who were the hardest to place in mainstream education were in the residential sector; thus many services focused their work on residential units.

The reasons why young people are looked-after are various. The official reasons identified by the Department of Health are: parents need relief; parents' health; child's welfare; no parents; homelessness; at child's request; offence; abuse/at risk; other. The largest category is that of 'abused/at risk' (45.4 per cent of the total in care as at 31 March 1994). Offenders represent a tiny proportion of the looked-after cohort – a mere 1.2 per cent. As a group, those looked-after represent some of the most damaged, troubled and abused children for whom the education system has to provide. It is probably true to say that all are victims – insofar as adults have failed to provide them with the sort of environment and nurturing which would enable them to develop into well-adjusted and secure young people – even if they appear to be the perpetrators of abuse or violence, or be 'out of control'. The research found that the perceptions of young people looked-after held by adults, particularly teachers, was a critical factor in the way in which they responded to education. It is thus important that the broad thrust of what some of these young people have experienced in their short lives is shared and that all those working with them realise the inestimable disadvantages that they have accumulated through no fault of their own.

What is problematic as regards the education of young people who are looked-after?

The problems have been well documented and they will only be outlined here; readers unfamiliar with them should seek the literature that has been referred to above. They will all be treated at length in later chapters as ways in which they are addressed are discussed. Those directly impinging upon educational experiences include the following:

- **fragmentation**: a variety of adults (for example, natural parents, relatives, foster carers, residential carers and social workers) hold information which is usually lodged with the natural parent(s) who have cared for the child continuously since birth; thus it is difficult to trace the history of young people's educational careers, strengths and weaknesses, interests and achievements.

- **changes of school**: young people who are not living consistently at home often have frequent changes of care placement which, for logistic or resource-driven reasons, may entail changes of school at times other than those 'normally' experienced – for example, other than at the end of a term or a school year, or at primary-secondary transfer stage. Children who very often lack social skills are faced with having to make new friends and establish relationships with new teachers far more frequently than their peers who may be better equipped to cope with this anyway.

- **poor attendance**: young people who are looked-after frequently have poor attendance records as a result of their out-of-school experiences; some come from homes where school is not valued or where the domestic situation militates against regular attendance and so irregular or minimal attendance has become routine; some have significant behaviour difficulties which mean that it is hard for them to maintain school placements; some may have periods out of school because of exclusion combined with changes of care placements.

- **low expectations**: very often adults working with young people who are looked-after have low expectations of what they can and/or will achieve at school, either because they consider that they are, by nature, low attainers, or because they consider that there are other things in their lives which take higher priority.

- **low attainment**: although there is a serious lack of reliable data about the attainment of these young people, what there are suggest that, without positive intervention and support, young people looked-after fail to attain in the 'normal' range in terms of 16+ public examinations.

It is, perhaps, important to stress at this stage that these 'problems' are largely contingent rather than inevitable. The research showed very clearly that when there is a high level of awareness of the potential problems among all those working with this group of young people, and when positive action is taken, the problems need not develop and can be dissolved. Although there is much to depress those engaged in this area, certainly in terms of the amount of very basic work that remains to be done and the developmental work which *could* be done, there is yet grounds for considerable optimism in that, as one service manager put it: 'If we had the resources, we could crack the problem; it is not insoluble'. It is hoped that the chapters which follow will give an indication of how this is done and 'find' many children. As one social worker put it: 'without the support service, there would be many more lost children'; while another referred to a young man who, when he came on the scene was 'a child who had given up' but who, with attention to his education, was able to enjoy a much more meaningful life.

Three key concepts in the education of children looked-after: Integration, Inclusion and Progression

The concepts of integration and inclusion were mentioned above as informing much of the ensuing report. These terms are more usually found in the discourse of special educational needs, where there is often theoretical debate about the distinction between them. In common parlance they are, in fact, used imprecisely and in practical terms there is interplay between them. However, very broadly, integration is used when the focus is on introducing pupils with special educational needs into an already existing environment and where uni- or bilateral (depending on the situation) adaptation is required; inclusion is used where the focus is on creating environments which are, *sui generis*, adaptive and able to accommodate whatever needs arise within the relevant community they serve. How are these concepts applied to the education of young people who are looked-after?

As regards *integration*, first, the data show that practitioners need to consider how to bring young people into contact with the culture and routines of school when, on account of their domestic experiences, these may be alien and incomprehensible. In the course of the research the following was cited.

> If from the age of three, you have been accustomed, at mid-day, to awakening your parents, who are sleeping off the previous night's hangover, and to receiving a volley of abuse on so doing, this is 'normal' experience for you by your early teens. You cannot then be expected to make a sudden switch to fit in with the rest of the world without a transitional period. It is entirely unrealistic for adults to expect you to get up one morning, clean and dressed in school uniform, to arrive at school in time and do a full day's work. You need to start with a part-time afternoon programme and gradually be 'integrated' into the sort of routines that others follow and accept as normal. These new, and previously unknown routines and the culture which they represent, need also to be integrated into your life style.

Thus, as in special education, 'integration' represented a process whereby it was possible for young people with particular, and usually very acute, needs to be embraced in what peers would regard as 'normal' society. Without this process, the young person remains alienated from the community which offers richer opportunities and empowers him/her to make choices about, and thus control, his/her future.

Second, the lives of young people need to be personally integrated. That care and education plans interacted in order to effect this integration was something which practitioners were increasingly realising and which was something that represented new findings from this research project. The awareness was not articulated at the time of the previous NFER research into the education of children in care. As one senior manager in a social services department put it:

> 'I came up via the residential route. I think that I was aware that you can have a marvellous care package but if education goes wrong, it is all hopeless ... In the past, you felt the effect of educational failure [ie, the care package collapsing] but didn't identify education as the critical element. I thought that education was something nice for them to do during the day – but not critical ... Now social workers identify education as a crucial element in the whole package – to make other things work ... you're doomed to failure without it.'

Third, in order for young people's lives to be *personally* integrated on an individual level, *services* had to be integrated. Inter-agency collaboration and joint working were essential. But these are notoriously difficult to achieve. Very obviously, as one senior manager pointed out, 'Social services deal with two per cent of the population and is very resource intensive here; the LEA deals with 100 per cent of the relevant population and resources are spread extensively'. There are thus very different priorities and ways of conceiving of clients. Another senior manager captured some of the tension when he said: 'Social services are responsible for vulnerable kids who are usually messing things up for schools'; and a further one said: 'There is political pressure to get shot of the kids we deal with'. The unique feature of the specialist education support services for children who are looked-after was the fact that they acted as a link between the social services and education departments: 'a bridge' or 'having a foot in both camps' were terms commonly applied – though one senior manager said, more pessimistically, that the service staff were 'between the devil and the deep blue sea'. The fact that inter-agency collaboration could be achieved where there was determination and clear management was borne out in the case studies. There was a clear view that, as one interviewee put it: 'The key challenge is the interface between the two agencies and how we achieve it without wasting energy in terms of who controls the service'.

As regards *inclusion*, the data show that certain attitudes are necessary in both schools and carers to maintain young people in school. There needs to be collaborative work and strategies, based on a common understanding of the situation, so that children can remain within the normal school community and gain access to the educational experiences to which they are entitled and which will give them access to a way of life alternative to, and offering richer opportunities than, the barren or abusive one which they have experienced prior to their being looked-after. Schools and carers need to work to enable young people looked-after to be 'included' in communities where they can receive what they are entitled to and would have received as a matter of course had they not had the domestic experiences which they have had, through no fault of their own.

The whole thrust of the chapters which follow is impelled by these notions of reparation and maintenance/sustenance. The evidence was that it is, essentially, a case of adults taking active responsibility for other adults' failures or deficiencies in order that further lives may not be broken; it is a matter of removing some of the burdens *from* young people, despite the fact that the hard everyday reality is that many of these young people present as 'burdens' to schools.

A third concept central to the education of looked-after young people is that of *progression*. A lot of social work involves planning: setting targets and then engaging in review. Young people have care plans – usually with the ultimate objective of returning them home or, if this is inappropriate, of settling them securely in an alternative home. As regards education, the concept of progression has been noticeably lacking. All the research evidence about usual practice has, until recently, suggested that mere attendance at school, or containment within the system, has been the primary focus of most attention given to education. Although attendance at school may mark a very real achievement for a young person who has been accustomed to regular truancy, it only marks the restoration of the opportunity to achieve within formal education. Once practice develops and those working with the young people consider achievement and attainment, then regard has to be given to progression on a broad front. What is the next step educationally and in terms of the young person's learning? How can the young people be moved on in educational terms of achievement on a day-to-day, week-by-week basis? Furthermore, what happens at the structured stages of transition: for example, from primary to secondary school, from key stage three to key stage four (when option choices for 16+ accreditation are made) and, particularly, what happens at the end of key stage four and the end of statutory schooling? It was no accident that several specialist support services were moving into post-16 work. If school education is promoted, it is irresponsible not to follow it through to further education and training (as most parents would do).

Connections with special education

It is mistaken to think that young people who are looked-after necessarily have special educational needs as defined by the Education Act 1993 – some looked-after children are academically successful and continue to higher education. However, a substantial number do present with special educational needs – particularly learning difficulties and emotional and behavioural difficulties. In this respect they should be treated as their peers and be subject to whatever procedures are in place in the school and the local authority in relation to the Code of Practice. The fact that they are looked-after is, in this respect, irrelevant.

However, it can be argued that they do merit special consideration by virtue of their looked-after status and the fact that they suffer disadvantage by the very nature of the consequences of their being looked-after – consequences which include the possibility of the 'problems' delineated above. In this respect, they have special needs. The needs arise from their 'care' environment rather than from the learning environment, as is the case with special educational needs.

There are strong links with the world of special education but the nature of these links should be clear. Many of the strategies of special education are relevant and effective with looked-after children – for example, the setting of small, viable targets; individual learning programmes within the necessary and supportive framework of a group situation; negotiated support mediated by all those who are working 'normally' with the child, including their peers; the use of counsellors or mentors to whom the young person can turn when things seem unmanageable; effective use of records; the celebration of any achievement, however slight. It is, thus, unsurprising that a number of looked-after pupils find an ally in the special needs co-ordinator. Where communication and co-operation were good, the child's life could be 'integrated' by, for example, a coherent pattern of statement and care reviews, and of individual education plans under the terms of the Code of Practice and of individual learning plans that were designed by social services teachers or care staff. It is not surprising that schools which had a reputation for their inclusiveness as regards pupils with special educational needs, found little difficulty in accommodating the needs of pupils who were looked-after.

Outline of report

The report starts by giving an overview of the national position regarding local authorities' provision and support for the education of young people 'looked after'. It then describes the work and organisation of discrete services for the support of the education of children looked-after, before considering the issue from the perspectives of carers and of schools. The final chapter attends to general issues and tries to draw out the principles which are relatable to the situation across authorities in England and Wales and, hypothetically, in other contexts; these lead to recommendations which expand upon those made by Ofsted/SSI and the DFEE.

CHAPTER 2
THE NATIONAL POSITION

This chapter presents data from the questionnaire on the education of looked-after children that was sent to all local authorities in England and Wales from a series of 'one-off' initial interviews that were conducted either face-to-face or on the telephone (14 authorities were visited in person and a further 13 contacted by telephone). In-depth case study data are reported in subsequent chapters.

The questionnaire responses

The questionnaire sought information on background details, services, training, policy development and statistical data relating to looked-after children. Responses were received from 66 authorities.

Identified LEA officer

Respondents were asked if there was an identified LEA officer responsible for looked-after children: 28 authorities affirmed that there was such an officer. Comments on the questionnaires made it clear that the responsibility was additional to a range of others, mainly related to special educational needs, and that post-holders already had an extremely demanding workload. This is unsurprising, given the decline in posts in LEA administration.

Twenty-four authorities reported that there was an identified committee responsible for the education of looked-after children. Comments suggested that what this meant in practice was that the issue arose within an existing forum such as Children's Services' Panel. On the one hand, this gives the opportunity for addressing the issue holistically, with a joint approach from services as appropriate; on the other, it can be neglected within a meeting that has been accustomed to a certain agenda and parameters of action.

Named teacher

Ofsted/SSI recommended that all schools should have an identified teacher holding responsibility for looked-after children; five authorities claimed that a list of these teachers was available. However, this may not have been comprehensive: other data suggested that there were problems here. LEAs were aware that a requirement for such a named person could result in resource implications as schools requested funding for an extra increment for the member of staff who assumed this responsibility. In some cases,

LEAs were trying to establish procedures for working with looked-after children through head teacher associations. This sometimes created difficulties in that not only did these meet only intermittently (usually termly) but, unsurprisingly, the item about looked-after pupils often came at the bottom of the agenda. The most positive action seemed to come from those authorities which had discrete support teachers regularly communicating with, and working in, schools. Even here, however, progress on the matter was patchy, although achieving a composite list remained a service aim. Where there was an identified teacher, it tended to be either the special needs co-ordinator or the teacher with responsibility for child protection.

Policy documents

Respondents were asked if there was a written policy regarding the education of looked-after children. Twenty-five respondents stated that there was such a policy, 36 stated that there was no policy, one did not know and there were four missing cases. Of the existing policies, three had been drawn up by the LEA, four by the social services department and 17 jointly (one missing case). The policies which were submitted as examples to the NFER, showed that there was much variety in their quality, scope and usefulness. This is discussed further below.

There were other joint policies in 16 authorities, mostly pertaining to transport or out-of-authority placement.

Joint meetings

Respondents were asked for details of meetings between personnel in the education and the social services departments which focused on looked-after children. These went on at all levels as is shown by table 2.1

Table 2.1 Frequency of meetings relevant to the education of looked-after children in responding authorities

	senior management	middle management	practitioner level
once or twice a year	11	5	0
every month/two months	20	27	9
weekly	1	2	10
missing cases	8	6	21
N	40	40	40

data based on 40 authorities responding to this question

Although there was no evidence of widespread joint meetings for this discrete issue, documentation submitted suggested that, where there was a high level of awareness of the needs of looked-after children, a high number of related meetings were perceived as germane to the issue. For example, the following multi-professional meetings were listed as relevant by one authority.

Authority level
- quarterly project meetings including officers from both departments
- bi-annual review of service level agreement between departments
- bi-annual EBD teachers' liaison at LEA level
- quarterly resource panel – SSD and LEA

Area level
- bi-annual project meetings
- termly tracking meetings
- monthly EBD network meetings

School level
- termly welfare meetings
- education planning meetings (fortnightly)

Project level
- weekly meetings to discuss referrals, admissions, pupil planning, review and tracking
- weekly meetings to plan and review provision

Provision for the education of looked-after children

Training

Fewer than half (28) the responding authorities stated that there was training with respect to the education of looked-after children available in the authority; 36 stated that there was no training available (two missing cases). Details of the recipients and providers of this training in the 28 authorities which offered it are given in tables 2.2 and 2.3 below. Joint training was only 'occasionally' engaged in in the majority of responding authorities.

Table 2.2   Groups to whom training regarding the education of looked-after children was available

group	LEAs
foster carers	14
residential care staff	19
social work teams	18
youth justice teams	7
teachers	15
governors	4
special needs support teams	9
other	3
n of cases	89

data based on 28 authorities responding to this question

Table 2.3   Providers of training for the education of looked-after children

provider	LEAs
LEA officer responsible for LAC	5
specialist support teachers for LAC	12
LEA learning support staff	12
social services officers	11
other	6

data based on 28 authorities responding to this question

Education posts

Of the responding authorities, 26 claimed to have education posts focused on looked-after children. Twenty of these authorities gave information as to the location of these teachers. In nine authorities they were confined to tuition in units attached to residential children's homes or secure accommodation; in eight authorities they provided both unit and home tuition; and in three, only home tuition. Funding for the posts was divided between departments: ten were funded by the social services department, eight were funded by the LEA (either discretely or as part of the learning support services) and seven were jointly funded (one missing case).

Twenty-four respondents specified the focus of the service. In 22 authorities, the focus was on children who were looked-after; 12 authorities had a wider brief for children and families at risk. The issues emerging from this will be discussed later in the report.

Management

In all cases but one, the teachers were managed by the department(s) which funded them: the exception was an LEA-funded post which was jointly managed.

Several of those engaged in the area had been seconded from, or were in, middle management positions. Having reviewed the situation obtaining in the authority, they had become acutely aware that effective policy and practice with regard to the education of looked-after children had considerable implications for wider policy and practice throughout the authority – in both education and social services departments – and required managing at a senior level. Although in some cases the practitioners involved had excellent support from line managers, elsewhere they considered that their line managers did not understand the issues and thus were not committed to effecting the necessary changes that support for the education of looked-after children required. In one case, the comment was made that the service 'lacks the confidence to promote its service, born out of confusion as to where it stands in the management structure'. As this is a relatively 'new' area, in some ways this misunderstanding is not surprising. However, there was evidence that the problems were associated with the broader one of ineffective channels of communication and collaboration between professional agencies. Both the Children Act 1989 and *the Code of Practice on the Identification and Assessment of Special Educational Needs* (DFE, 1994), which relates to part III of the Education Act 1993 (part IV of the Education Act 1996), promote, in strong terms, the necessity for inter-agency co-operation and, *per se*, are the heirs of a long line of official reports stressing the same need – for example, the Seebohm Report (1968) and the Warnock Report (1978). Those trying to enhance the education of looked-after children were, thus, apparently working in an alien environment which was not conducive to the type of practice required and in which this practice had little precedent. As one interviewee put it: 'the organisation has the problems, not the kids'.

Organisational problems

Practitioners encountered a depressingly long list of broad organisational problems, which, arguably, needed recognition and action by senior management. It should be pointed out that these problems were over and above those emanating from negative attitudes, such as 'tarring all looked-after children with the same brush' and perceiving the young people as 'the problem' rather than trying to alleviate the difficulties which had been thrust on them by virtue of domestic situations not of their making. These problems were, also, over and above those emerging from the general social and political environment – for example, competition between schools making them 'image-conscious' and reluctant to accept pupils perceived as difficult or 'undesirable' by other parents. Although it is, of course, extremely difficult to 'prove' discrimination, in that data chiefly come from those discriminated against rather than the discriminators, the case study work in the NFER project collected evidence, from social workers, service workers and carers, of discrimination towards looked-after children not only from schools but also from other parents – for example, by 'threats' to the head teacher if a 'difficult' child remained at the school and telling their own children not to associate with their looked-after peer(s).

Other specific problems included low staff morale and the complex behavioural difficulties of young people within residential children's homes. A number of authorities were seeking to address fundamental problems in the management of residential homes. There was evidence from the NFER case studies that such problems had to be resolved before an environment conducive to education could be established.

The list of broad organisational problems reported by questionnaire respondents and those participating in the initial interview programme variously included:

- unduly heavy caseloads leaving time neither for proactive liaison nor for in-service training and awareness raising – the latter was vital, particularly where there was a high turnover of social workers;

- confusion and dislocation caused by purchaser/provider splits;

- blurred boundaries of service provision and confusion as to its role (e.g. expectations of behaviour modification or alternative education);

- defensive rather than collaborative professional attitudes (the *quality* of personnel was not considered a problem) and resistance to change;

- ill-defined roles for 'units' such as Observation and Assessment Centres (social services) or Pupil Referral Units (education);

- inadequate provision and placements for young people whose needs had been identified – resulting in congestion in the system and young people remaining in inappropriate provision and/or service provision being a 'last stop';

- poor communication, resulting in the 'invisibility' of, and/or misunderstanding about, any educational services for looked-after children;

- departmental management information systems which were not only incompatible across departments (and sometimes within them) but were also not designed to yield information relevant and essential to enhancing the education of looked-after children – professionals were 'living on part knowledge of cases';

- absence of monitoring systems generating data helpful for the planning of provision;

- reluctance of education departments to alienate/aggravate schools by making demands – for example, that each had a named person for looked-after children;

- the social services policy of minimal intervention effecting a situation in which education was often in crisis before support was sought – 'referrals are usually made at the point of crisis, which is usually too late';

- social workers reluctant to engage with education professionals – 'bringing their own baggage to cases';

- difficulties in education support services gaining access to the Age-Weighted Pupil Unit (AWPU) of an excluded pupil even where these services were the sole or primary source of education for that pupil;

- the limited hours and variable quality of home tuition – there was a concern that home tutors were often insensitive to, and inadequate for, the particular needs of looked-after children;

- problems of access to grant maintained schools;

- service level agreements restricting access – for example, to the educational psychology service and other specialist services;

- different profiles of support services within the education department – for example, the stage at which schools could secure advice from the authority's behaviour support team (if there was one);

- the absence of discrete budgets resulting in any service provision for the education of looked-after children being subject to competing priorities;

- lack of clerical support.

Respondents spoke of working around and with existing systems, and of the necessity of ensuring the viability of any initiatives within established frameworks, particularly in the light of the unlikelihood of significant additional resources to support the education of looked-after children in the present context of financial stringency. The detailed NFER research (reported in subsequent chapters) showed that individual case work alone was ineffective unless there were substantial attitudinal and practical changes throughout education and social services departments. First, where pump-priming or time-limited money had been allocated to the education of looked-after children, the survival of any effective practice thereby established stood or fell, when discrete posts were removed on the withdrawal of funding, by the degree to which that practice was embedded in regular routines. Second, the effective support of the education of looked-after children entailed an awareness and management of the contribution of other professionals such as learning or behaviour support teachers, education welfare officers, educational psychologists and home tutors. All this required not only a high level of management skills in the heads of the education support services and their staff but also a 'managerially aware' environment in which these people could function: the way for them to 'facilitate' had, in turn, to be cleared. The evidence pointed to the fact that this was very much a 'whole authority' issue and needed addressing at all levels within organisational structures.

The task of working with the existing systems was clearly easier in some authorities than in others. In some, there were determined efforts to break down the barriers, acknowledge the problems and begin, albeit slowly, to address them; in others, the problems were perceived as insurmountable – at least at the time of the research and with current budgets – and there were moves which further exacerbated the situation.

These moves were diverse in origin. For example, in one authority, there had been an education social worker who worked solely with looked-after children; this post had been GEST-funded but was removed when funding was withdrawn, rather than becoming embedded in base funding. In a second example, the questionnaire response had indicated that substantial action was imminent by way of establishing an authority database of children in need and reviewing procedures and practice on a corporate basis. However, since the return had been made, the social services department had been subject to a 25 per cent budget cut, extensive reorganisation, reduction in administrative support and the relocation of social workers. The education of looked-after children 'remained a priority' but the planned action had not been realised. In a third authority, a respondent from social services referred to his reluctance to work too closely with education colleagues because of 'the problem of language and stereotypical views'. How these problems can be overcome without people getting to know and understand each other's *modus operandi* is unclear.

There was also evidence that in some authorities, where posts had been created or, at least, secondments sanctioned, for someone to engage with the issue of the education of looked-after children, insufficient thought had been given to the focus of the work. In one incident, for example, time was wasted 'searching for cases' among the looked-after population. The post had been created essentially to work with young people of a particular age but, once the post-holder started work, it was found that the core of the problem had been erroneously located. Elsewhere, post-holders had very vague job descriptions, received little direction from senior managers as to what exactly they were expected to do and had not had the benefit of any management training. It is a tribute to the commitment and resourcefulness of some of these post-holders that they achieved a considerable amount against the odds.

A shire county had an established team of support services working with looked-after children but the management of the team had been, and was, insecure. Thus the teachers, although individually experienced in the field, encountered difficulties accessing services and particular schools, disseminating good practice and getting themselves known to colleagues whom they could support. There was a lack of understanding about the role of the team: for example, whether they represented extra teachers or facilitators – an issue which arose, and was variously answered, in other authorities.

Positive initiatives – some examples

In a few authorities there were some very positive and purposeful initiatives designed to overcome some of what had been identified as problematic. Some examples follow; these are additional to the case studies presented in subsequent chapters.

One inner London borough had drawn up a joint action plan, led by Assistant Directors of the education and social services departments; they were considering integrating this into the borough's mandatory Children's Services Plan. The plan addressed the following issues:

- data management
- the placement planning process
- inter-borough placements
- procedures for special educational needs – for example, the possibility of joint care and statement reviews
- the maintenance of school placements when care placements change
- roles and responsibilities – for example, carer contribution and training
- indicators for action – for example, poor attendance, exclusion
- 'double triggers' – for example, the exclusion of a pupil who was looked-after.

The authority was trying to redirect monies made available by a change of policy from residential to community provision and were hoping to develop joint strategies to avoid duplication of intervention and thus save money (for example, with respect to pupils with emotional and behavioural difficulties). The respondent in this authority pointed out that initiative with regard to looked-after children had to be seen in the context of a clutch of mutually interacting initiatives within the borough.

A second London borough had also agreed a joint education/social services policy; good relations with the school inspection team meant that the implementation of this policy could be monitored and supported centrally. A nominated person had been established in a third of the borough's schools – although it was acknowledged that this was 'a long job' and too much pressure could not be brought to bear on schools. There had also been clarification of expectations made of carers and social workers (procedures for liaison – who does what, when and so forth).

A third London borough, influenced by the Audit Commission (1994) report, had established a jointly funded post for work with schools and carers of excluded children looked-after within the borough (the initiative could not, at the time, be extended to the many children looked-after by the authority but fostered outside the borough). A data base was being established as was training for foster carers and social workers in children's services and fostering teams. The immediately identified issues were:

- sharing of information
- ensuring school prospectuses were available to relevant personnel within social services
- designing basic information sheets about looked-after children
- discussing venues for meetings (to ensure relevant attendance)

In a metropolitan authority, looked-after children had been the responsibility of the hospital education service. However, it had become apparent that 'being in a residential children's home equalled being out of school' and there were problems about teachers in the hospital service getting access to looked-after children. A working party was thus set up and two teachers were appointed, resourced by corporate Children Act money plus collaborative funding from the social services department, education department and health authority. The role of the teachers included counselling, negotiating placements, preparing an education programme for those young people for whom school was not perceived to be an option, and raising awareness of educational issues in residential children's homes. A further development was that the needs of looked-after children were given priority within the authority's initiatives for disaffected, poor attending and excluded pupils. It was, thus, claimed that the discrete work (a small part of which continued) had become embedded in regular practice. However, the disadvantage was that if they did not present with any particular problems at school, looked-after children got no particular attention paid to their education (other than what social workers or carers might do) and were not monitored separately. The situation was under review.

In a second metropolitan authority, the Ofsted/SSI report had been the catalyst for change – although 'people were talking about it before'. A joint policy document was issued. Its purposes were:

- to ensure that children who are looked-after gain a higher profile in order that the educational disadvantage typically experienced can be properly addressed;
- to underline the commitment of education and social services to joint working, in order that the educational needs of children who are looked-after are assessed, provided for and reviewed;
- to establish, in principle, the roles and responsibilities of those involved in either providing the day-to-day education and care of the children or those who have a duty to support the education and care of the children;
- to establish a framework within which services can develop within education and social services in order that the children themselves receive better co-ordinated support.

Two secondments, one from the education department and one from social services, were made, originally for six months. Assistant directors of both departments were actively involved and the project was joint funded. The task of the secondees was to implement policy at strategic and operational levels throughout the authority. The policy was set within the framework of the Integrated Services Plan (social services, education and health), there was member support and a project steering group with broad representation. The secondees engaged in awareness raising and prompted action at all officer levels and with carers and schools. The chief aim was to identify and clarify the locus of responsibilities. As one of the secondees said: 'no one thinks it is right that children are out of school in residential care but no one sees it as their responsibility to do anything about it'.

A third metropolitan authority specified that 'every effort should be made':

- to maintain continuity of schooling;
- to keep regular contact with the child's school and other relevant educational services;
- to provide a placement that both encourages and stimulates a child to develop and learn;
- to understand any difficulties that may be causing the child to reject or under-achieve at school;
- to give school attendance problems and their resolution a high priority;
- to ensure that a child from an ethnic minority community receives an education that assists her/him in reaching an understanding and knowledge of his/her own history;
- to encourage young people to consider staying on at school or attending further education.

A shire county had drawn up a service level agreement between the education and social services departments. This was guided by a set of principles, one of which stated:

Young people looked after by the local authority are entitled to education and care provision which prepares them for adulthood and citizenship by a) affording them opportunities to achieve success and b) offering positive alternatives to the disrupted educational placements and damaging personal histories which many have experienced.

Schools were required to ensure that staff were aware of the particular educational disadvantages of young people looked-after; to produce an education plan (linked to any Individual Education Plan which the pupil might have under the terms of the Code of Practice and also his/her care plan under the terms of the Children Act 1989); and to appoint a named teacher for each pupil looked-after. The particular responsibilities of the LEA support service for pupils with emotional and behavioural difficulties and of the education welfare service were also stated: these included supporting schools in meeting needs, in admitting, integrating and including these pupils, in staff development related to looked-after children and in the development of effective communication with the social services department. Looked-after children without a school place were the responsibility of one of the support services who would draw up an education plan for them. Social services staff were required, *inter alia*, to provide key workers to liaise with education staff for children in community homes; inform the school and appropriate LEA officer of care placement moves; and avoid changes in school placements wherever possible.

A Welsh authority, visited prior to its reorganisation, articulated one of its current strategic aims as follows:

to work with children's homes, helping children and young people enjoy personal success in education by:

- ensuring that each child has a named person responsible for the education component of his/her care plan
- ensuring that each child has a regularly updated educational profile in his/her file
- ensuring that each child has a clear education support plan which is evaluated at least every term
- the officer in charge and the support teacher holding a twice yearly meeting to review all aspects of the children's education
- helping children's homes to create a positive educational environment and to develop educational resources
- working with the staff in homes to raise their confidence and keep them informed of relevant educational legislation
- providing practical support to schools.

Individual authorities were working with voluntary organisations to review practice. In one case, a group of neighbouring authorities had, with a voluntary organisation, established a project focused on residential care. A similar initiative, working with a further group of authorities and the same voluntary organisation (though with a different project officer), was being implemented at the time of this report going to press. The extent to which it built on knowledge gained from its predecessor in order to develop practice, rather than do the same thing somewhere else, was not clear.

Policy documents

The policy documentation submitted by local authorities ranged from general broad statements of intent, to more specific requirements on professional groups, to focused action plans. Some originated with the education support services themselves while others had been drawn up by multi-professional working parties. The origin was salient to their scope and usefulness. On the one hand, if they were at too broad a level, they could be too general as there was no intimate understanding of the particular issues; on the other, they could be too insular, with practitioners too immersed in their own concerns and failing to see the wider issues on which these impinged and depended for their resolution. Some were, clearly, more by way of an attempt to put boundaries round responsibilities for financial reasons rather than to ensure that positive action was taken: one policy statement focused entirely on finance (which department was responsible for what provision) and respective provision stating that 'it is not the role of the social services department to compensate for a lack of educational provision by reception into care or other means' and 'it is not the role of the education department to compensate for a lack of appropriate social services provision or support to families by placements in residential schools'. Although this needs to be said, *qua* policy document on the education of looked-after children, it is slight and adversarial rather than something facilitating joint provision. There is, perhaps, a difference between making clear to professional colleagues what their responsibilities are and coming together to provide something that is, essentially, 'greater than its parts'. Another policy document gave evidence of trying to do the latter (in a range of contexts), as the following excerpts illustrate:

> - The LEA will seek to co-ordinate arrangements between schools and social services to ensure that effective systems and processes are in place for promoting the educational attainment of children being looked after.
> - The LEA will offer assistance to schools and social services whenever agreed care and education plans require additional support or special services.

- The LEA shares the corporate parenting role of the local authority for children being looked after and therefore will seek to support social services in securing appropriate educational experiences for these children.
- Regular communication and good partnerships between school and care providers should reduce the need to exclude children, or failing that, to ensure that it is done in a planned and co-ordinated way.
- Performance indicators will be developed by education and social services to monitor the effectiveness of the process.

Another authority took the first step by acknowledging that there were incipient problems:

> Funding mechanisms for local councils traditionally result in compartmentalisation of budgets and consequent lack of flexibility. This can have a serious effect when deciding which directorate should pay for placements. Frequently the problems experienced by families and the educational needs of children within the families are intermingled. Good practice demands close liaison between departments at an early stage of identification of need in order to best meet the needs of the child. DFE circular 9/94 alludes to the possibility of local authorities creating a joint fund for common cases which eliminates the current common practice of 'horse trading' between departments.

One metropolitan authority, not included in the examples above, had decided on strategic planning at all levels but in clear, basic areas: it sought data on what was required in residential care as regards training, the role of the residential social worker, resources (for example, computers and library facilities in residential homes) and the positive use – perhaps redirection – of existing resources (for example, the purchase of newspapers from budgets for personal allowances and clothing).

An inner London borough had made a clear statement of joint policy, with corporate commitment – extracts are as follows:

- The borough is committed to the provision of a quality service to all children and young people looked after by the local authority and to ensuring that every child's educational needs, including any special educational needs, are met whilst being provided with accommodation.
- Children and young people looked after by the local authority have the same right to education as all children and young people.

- The Council and schools will work together to promote educational achievement and to ensure an appropriate educational placement and entitlement for children looked after by the local authority in accordance with the statutory requirements and the joint SSI/Ofsted standards.
- Consideration will be given in placement planning to the contribution the placement makes to meeting the child's educational needs, including the need for continuity of education
- The care plan will be prepared following consultation with Education, the child's school and teacher and having taken account of specialist advice from others who could make an appropriate contribution.

The borough was to maintain an education plan for every child looked-after and was to secure a designated teacher in all its schools. Interestingly, the policy was supported by a set of procedures which made reference to existing relevant procedures. This linking of policy and procedures, and the linking of procedures in different policy areas in order to ensure coherence, though logical and managerially critical, is often lacking. It was particularly strong in some of the case study authorities reported in subsequent chapters. The procedures in the authority discussed above included those for gathering information about the child's school career (in order to inform the care plan) – for example, whether the child had an individual education plan under the Education Act 1993, or a record of achievement. Educational records of all looked-after children were to be held by one education officer (thus providing opportunities for an overview and monitoring) who was responsible for disseminating relevant information to other support services such as those for learning support or the Educational Welfare Service (thus giving the opportunity for coherence of support).

Of the local authority documents not cited above, some were merely admissions criteria for support while other 'policies' were very limited in scope – relating, for example, to transport arrangements or '52 week' placements in out-authority residential institutions. The policy documents gave messages about the authority's approach to looked-after children – messages which related to issues explored in subsequent chapters of this report. For example, did the policy relate only to those looked-after children whose education presented grave difficulties – such as those excluded or exhibiting extreme behavioural difficulties; or did it acknowledge that all looked-after children were, potentially, educationally vulnerable and that monitoring and evaluation was needed across the whole group, if only by way of expectations of carers?

Monitoring and evaluation

In the majority of cases, it was not immediately clear how the general statements of policy were monitored or evaluated. That there were many good intentions was not in doubt; how they were to be realised in practical terms was. There was evidence that it may be that some authorities found it difficult, in management terms, to move on from the 'awareness raising' stage.

One authority was unusual in embarking upon a phased project which included the assessment of needs and the delivery of a training programme to meet these. The assessment was undertaken by specialists from a local authority which had had greater experience with the education of looked-after children, working in collaboration with senior managers, staff of residential children's homes, foster carers, head teachers and governors, and young people in residential care. The resulting report was to 'provide the information necessary to structure an appropriate training and support programme designed to meet identified needs and to achieve the overall aim of the proposal'. The training was to be in the form of a series of one-day awareness raising/basic training days for residential, field and education social workers; foster carers; designated teachers and school governors. This was to be followed by two 36 hour comprehensive training programmes. The project was to be evaluated by senior managers and participants and outcomes measured against pre-determined performance indicators.

Small-scale research/data collection exercises

A few authorities gave evidence of small-scale research/monitoring exercises which they had conducted internally: for example, on the position regarding exclusion on a single 'snapshot' day. These exercises were sometimes prompted by the Ofsted/SSI report.

The most comprehensive of the exercises for which documentation was submitted to the NFER involved a metropolitan borough's questionnaire to its schools eliciting data on:

- how well informed schools were about which children are looked-after;
- the accuracy of the information received from social services;
- the school's management systems and strategies for meeting the needs of children looked-after;

- the educational attainment of each child looked-after;
- any special educational needs that the child might have;
- the extent to which an educational partnership had been achieved with social services and the child's carers;
- the work-related curriculum (secondary schools only).

In addition, an attendance survey of looked-after children was carried out.

Key issues were recommended as a result of the investigation, involving action from the education department, social services, schools and carers.

It was noticeable that the collection and publication of hard data about the position regarding the education of looked-after children was often the impetus for action; this highlights the position on the other side of the coin, whereby lack of specific policy and practice is often on account of 'ignorance' and lack of knowledge rather than dismissal of cogent evidence. This is, in turn, reflected at national level: the previous chapter explained how the whole issue of the education of children in care was brought firmly onto the agenda by a researcher's identification of the lack of literature and knowledge about the area. In many cases, the evidence, once collected and presented, was too powerful for 'corporate parents' to ignore – at least, in principle, even if the development of practice was perceived as a formidable business.

Pilot studies

Although, as has been stated above, whole-authority change involved awareness and action at all levels of management across departments, there was evidence that an effective agency for change could be a pilot or feasibility study. This was probably a particularly useful strategy where additional resources were minimal. The pilot schemes were focused, in some cases, on a particular group of young people – for example, in a defined age group or a residential resource; at others, on a particular initiative – for example, an inner London and a northern metropolitan authority had each established a 'book-buying'/literature/literacy scheme (see Menmuir, 1994; Bald et al., 1995). The advantages of pilot studies were considered to be their 'containability' and the fact that a project cycle could be seen through and evaluated. Following this, the messages from the work could be related more widely within the authority. This extension was assisted by the ready evidence of its viability and advantages to practitioners; there was the possibility that those involved would act as its advocates and ambassadors to colleagues – a factor which has proven effectiveness in the wider application of change. A pilot could also demonstrate where extension was not appropriate; it had the advantage that it had a 'shelf-life' and could serve a function as a developmental phase, rather than necessarily providing a blueprint for future provision. As following chapters will show, in those authorities where support for the education of looked-after children was more mature, a definite cycle of development would be discerned, whereby when groups of people were trained they were able to take responsibility for a task, leaving the specialist team free to move on elsewhere.

However, the disadvantages were that pilot initiatives could fail to extend across the authority, remain confined to a particular geographical area, and be ignored by senior management so implications were not identified and followed up. This led to a situation in which there was tremendous inter- and intra-authority unevenness of provision, so that a young person's chances of having serious and informed attention paid to his/her educational career depended on where s/he happened to live. The NFER research showed that although there are signs of positive practice as regards the education of looked-after children, there are equally strong signs that too much is left to chance.

Another aspect of this 'chance' reveals itself where there is trans-authority fostering – particularly acute in metropolitan boroughs. One authority was starting to support the education of its looked-after children who were resident in the borough but did not extend this to the considerable proportion of its looked-after children who were in residential or foster care outside the borough. The rationale was that while it was valuable to establish good relations with carers and the borough's own schools, it was not a justifiable use of scarce resources to build up similar relationships with another borough's schools. The upshot of this was that looked-after young people were discriminated against if placed outside the borough. The NFER project case study work revealed similar 'ownership' difficulties when 'receiving' authorities – fostering and educating young people from a neighbouring borough – seemed reluctant to promote their cause. In the particular cases which came to light in the research, the young people concerned were entirely dependent on the advocacy of their carer. There must be many cases where they do not have this to depend on. The situation would seem to warrant further investigation.

All these manifestations of 'chance' raise hard questions about not only the notion of 'corporate parenting' but also the articulation of the concept of 'parental partnership'. In recent legislation, parents have been given an increasing voice in education (for example, the right to state a preference for their child's school, representation on governing bodies, expectations of consultation and involvement if their child has special educational needs) and the corpus of research literature agrees that pupils thrive educationally where their parents support their education. It is presently unclear how these concepts and 'entitlements' transfer when parenting is 'corporate' and, indeed, how within the 'corporation' as it were, different voices – such as those of the natural parents – are heard. There are basic challenges not only to local authorities as a whole, who are legally 'looking after' the young people, but also to schools with regard to their home–school policies and practice, and many other professional groups.

Detailed statistical data on the education of looked-after children

Authorities were asked to give information about the numbers of looked-after children, of their school placement and of looked-after children with special educational needs. They were also asked whether data about particular relevant issues (for example, exclusions, attainment, changes of placement) could be extracted from centrally held records (rather than case files or service records of children who were clients).

The responses were disappointing in terms both of response rates and of the data that could be supplied. Few respondents stated that data were held in this way. Comments both on the questionnaire and, especially, in interviews, indicated that the fragmentation referred to in chapter one was a very real issue as regards data collection. While individual LEAs would, of course, have details on pupils with statements, they rarely had a marker which could generate a list of those who were looked-after. Similarly, social services had lists of looked-after children but no marker to indicate which of those had a statement or needed learning support. Data were often not kept inclusively: they might, for example, be available for young people in residential care but not for those in foster care; or they might be kept for those young people referred to the teaching support service, but not for others for whom there were no ostensible 'problems'. Again, the existence and maintenance of data might depend on individual social work teams. In several authorities, the response was that the data 'should be' kept by one department or the other, but the implication was not only that it might not necessarily be kept but also that there was no use made of it, or monitoring of it, at authority level. Although there is no suggestion that individual social workers did not keep meticulous records of young people's educational careers, this does not help strategic planning on a departmental basis. Although individual files seemed to be improved in terms of educational data since the previous NFER research (Fletcher-Campbell and Hall, 1990), there was little evidence that the overall position at local authority level was much improved.

The education department in one metropolitan borough, under the general aim 'to raise the standard of educational achievement of all children and young people looked after by the borough', had identified the following objectives with respect to the collection of hard data:

i)   to identify numbers of young people looked-after under categories (e.g. legal status, type of placement);

ii)   to identify educational provision for these pupils;

iii)   to identify baseline numbers of exclusions, staying-on rates post-16, exam results, entry to higher education;

iv)   to create a database for the above.

This database having been established, the department had identified how it was to be used and had formulated the following related objectives:

v)   to create a reporting system to monitor (iii);

vi)   to ensure that all children and young people of statutory school age are receiving education;

vii)   to decrease exclusion rates by 10%;

viii)   to increase staying-on rate post-16 by 10%;

ix)   to increase exam success by 10%;

x)   to report to the directorate management teams in education and social services.

Conclusions

From the evidence available, it would seem that there is a reasonable degree of awareness that the education of young people who are looked-after can pose problems and needs discrete scrutiny. Given the statements from the DFE (1994) and Ofsted/SSI (1994) this should hardly be surprising. However, in only a few cases did this seem to be connected to the notion of corporate parenting. Perhaps, indeed, this is a manifestation of a vicious circle. A mature understanding of corporate care (that is, something that is managed and explicitly articulated, rather than being a composite of individuals all doing their best) is needed for young people in the care system to maximise the opportunities offered by education; concomitantly, this area is one where the immediate task-at-hand has been clearly identified (in default of effective practice) and, if tackled, a notion of what corporate parenting is can be derived from the practice – and then extended to other neglected and problematic areas such as health and employment opportunities for this group of young people. Although there were some very valuable initiatives in place in a number of authorities, yet there was less evidence that they were likely to become embedded in all the relevant working practices, affect management structures and be part of routine cycles of monitoring, evaluation and review. It should also be pointed out that returns were only received from about half of all LEAs in England and Wales (the figures are for the position prior to local government reorganisation – ie when there were 117 local authorities). It could reasonably be inferred that those authorities which did not respond (despite two follow-up reminder letters) were not active in the area; there was evidence that those authorities which had established initiatives were keen to share practice and were 'visible and vocal' within networks. There is, thus, still a long way to go.

To end on a more optimistic note, 51 of the 66 authorities responding to the NFER questionnaire stated that they had plans to develop initiatives to support the education of looked-after children in the future (eight gave a negative response to this question and there were seven missing cases). The concern emerging from the research data was that developments would only succeed if they were managed at a whole-authority level; in only a few cases did this seem to be likely.

Summary

♦ Less than a half (28) of the 66 local education authorities which responded to the NFER questionnaire had an LEA officer with identified responsibility for the education of looked-after children; in all cases, this responsibility was additional to a wide range of other responsibilities, commonly relating to special educational needs;

♦ there was no evidence that the recommendation of Ofsted and SSI that schools have a named person responsible for looked-after pupils has been widely implemented;

♦ in 25 responding authorities there was a written policy regarding the education of looked-after children; the majority of these had been drawn up jointly by the education and social services departments;

♦ 26 authorities claimed to have discrete teaching posts for looked-after children; the majority of these posts were jointly resourced and managed by education and social services departments;

- there was a wide range of managerial and organisational problems faced by personnel involved in supporting the education of looked-after children; most of these were a function of inflexible professional boundaries, lack of experience in inter-professional collaboration, and poor information management;

- a few authorities had made positive and purposeful initiatives designed to overcome some of what had been identified as problematic; these ranged from small-scale 'pilot' or time-limited schemes to the wider scrutiny of existing practice throughout the authority;

- the nature and quality of documentation varied widely from broad statements of intent or principles, to more focused action plans;

- rigorous monitoring and evaluation seemed to be neglected in many cases, often because the locus of professional responsibility was unclear; however, some authorities had undertaken small-scale research and evaluation exercises which were useful in policy review;

- few authorities kept centralised records of such data as the educational placement or progress of looked-after children; although these data did, of course, exist, they were not readily accessible or in a form useful for planning overall support for young people looked-after;

- a substantial number (51) of responding authorities stated that they had plans to develop services to support the education of young people looked-after.

CHAPTER 3
THE SOCIAL SERVICES' EDUCATION SUPPORT SERVICES
– STAFF, USERS, AIMS & PRINCIPLES

There was various terminology for the discrete services which some local authorities had established; in order to preserve confidentiality, so that quotations are not attributable to particular services, the general term 'education support services' will be used in this chapter and those following. This chapter will describe the policy and rationale of these services, their staffing and their clients. The data are based on the six case study authorities, each of which had a discrete team of teachers for the educational support of young people looked-after.

The organisation and management of the services

The size of the services, in relation to the relevant school and care population, varied, largely on account of: historic circumstances (e.g. whether the service had been formed by redeployment, after a pilot scheme), funding arrangements, and brief (for whom the service was intended). Each of these will be discussed later.

Very obviously, the services were paid for either by social services or by the local education authority. In some cases, and this was reinforced by other data presented in chapter two, the funding was explicitly joint and there could also be implicit subsidy from one or other departments, by the provision of a site or a capitation or training allowance, for example. The largest services were funded by social services. Their perceived success had largely, not though entirely, negated persistent questioning about the logic of social services employing teachers: put baldly – Should not the education department contain its own problems? Ironically, their success also made the services very attractive propositions for education departments struggling to provide for excluded pupils and those with emotional and behavioural difficulties. There are related resourcing issues which will be discussed in chapter seven.

It is a mere truism to point out that arguments about resourcing will persist unabated in any political context, especially where there is overall financial stringency imposed either by the local or the national government. That demand for welfare services exceeds supply is, probably, inevitable rather than contingent. This chapter will not enter the intricacies of local politics. The critical issue is to provide, in some shape or form, the type of support which the services provided. It will be seen that the *sui generis* characteristic of the support was its bridging between the two departments. From which side the funding comes is, to a certain extent, immaterial and may more appropriately and properly be decided on a local rather than national basis. Different local contexts, which bring with them a history and tradition of certain patterns of provision, may make one arrangement sensible in one area and another arrangement sensible in another. The important thing is that certain outcomes or standards are guaranteed: democratic processes must decide how best to design the administrative mechanisms. It ought, however, to be pointed out that uncertainty as regards a service's future could be damaging. This is a local authority issue involving inter-agency and inter-departmental debate about the corporate parent role. It is, perhaps, unfortunate that the DFE/DoH (1994) joint circular focused more on institutional than local government arrangements. Work in related areas (such as Joint Services Plans, see for example SSI, 1994) may provide much that is of relevance to the higher level management of the education of looked-after children.

Initiation of the services

There was a common pattern through the case study authorities as to how the services were originally established. This was largely because these services were amongst the 'oldest'; more recent initiatives have been prompted by catalysts such as the Ofsted/SSI (1995) report and have, thus, a different history, as was described in chapter two. It is not relevant to report the history of the services other than to refer to the implications for present policy and practice and also for other authorities which may be considering taking similar measures. Briefly, the services generally arose in one of two ways, both of which have been referred to in chapter two. First, they were born out of the closure of Community Homes with Education (CHEs) or education units attached to residential children's homes. Staff either took retirement or redundancy, or were redeployed to completely new posts in the newly formed support services. The impact of the latter cannot be underestimated: in many of the early examples, staff development was negligible and staff had, simply, to find their feet in their new role. Having been used to working with a very few difficult young people every day in one site, they now found themselves working with a range of adults in social services and education at various management levels, and having to work in a supportive, facilitating role as much as, or more than, directly with young people. It is unsurprising that some staff left; it is extremely surprising, given all that is known about the management of change and the necessity for accompanying staff development, that the new services flourished as they did. The fact that they did flourish, to the extent that, only a few years later, encomia were coming thick and fast (see the end of this chapter) is to the inestimable credit of those who led the services in the early days and to the staff who made the change so ably. The second way in which services arose was by way of a pilot scheme or a smaller-scale initiative which, having been shown to be be viable, was adopted more widely.

It is true that interviewees remarked that in the early stages roles and responsibilities were often unclear; this reflects, probably, the uncertain management and organisational position of the services. Although paid for by social services, accountability was often to the education department, by whom the teachers were actually employed. The new services were new species, related to but more complex than the education department's general learning support teams. The history of the latter is well documented – following the Education Act 1981 many remedial teachers found themselves in a similar position of no longer working with individual pupils, but having to advise colleagues and facilitate the pupils' learning within the mainstream classroom. But special needs teachers rarely have contact with the range of professionals and practitioners that the social services education support teachers have. The implications of the role for training and recruitment will be considered in chapter seven.

In best practice, the initial confusion about roles and responsibilities had been eliminated. Services had clear policies, line management and referral policies. In some cases these differed between area teams while in others there was the same approach throughout the authority. Interference with the latter was caused by factors in the policy context: for example, the actual and potential proportion of grant maintained schools (which had a different impact in different authorities) and, at the time of the research, local government reorganisation. Other factors causing differences in service approaches included the geographical location – for example, whether it was a large, widely dispersed shire county or a compact metropolitan one; and the amount of staff hours available. Figures about time available are not entirely helpful in that services had different briefs and accepted referrals from different client groups – see below.

The staff

Before what the staff actually did is described in more detail, a note on the staff profile might be timely. 'Variety' was the principal descriptor. Often, the 'oldest' members of the teams had, as stated above, been redeployed from social services' on-site education units. But the previous history of these teachers was equally varied: some had come from mainstream schools, some from special education, some had specialised in teaching pupils with emotional and behavioural difficulties. All these features were represented in the overall staff teams. Although, as stated above, staff mostly worked with secondary school aged pupils, team leaders commented that the overall staffing could offer both primary and secondary school experience, mainstream and special, and, generally, cover the National Curriculum – though, as one interviewee said, 'but that's not what our work is about'. The characteristics of flexibility, the ability to work with a wide range of adults, and the ability to move easily between social services and education environments, were of greater salience than any particular background.

The staff were, certainly initially, untrained. The rapidity with which individuals learnt on the job was referred to by some users of the service. Their engagement in the staff development training of others will be reported below. Their own staff development was often unsystematic. In some cases, the staff had access to the LEA INSET programme but resources were extremely limited and might only resource two or three staff to attend an external one-day course. Staff were keen to keep in touch with mainstream curriculum developments but often found themselves leading, rather than receiving, training for new initiatives – for example, the Code of Practice – because they had taken on the task of briefing social services colleagues or because they were facilitating colleagues' management of young people rather than doing it directly themselves (see below). In many ways, the training needs of staff centred round management issues – working with adults, negotiation and advocacy. Managers were open-minded about new appointments but most favoured those with mainstream experience – on the grounds that they had to have credibility in mainstream schools. One senior member of a team remarked that it was not a job for newly-qualified teachers – it was far too stressful and 'demanded 100 per cent all the time – you can easily get burn-out'. In one authority, where there were restraints on new appointments, the service manager was appointing to the team, as a pilot exercise, a residential social worker. It was considered that, as there was less and less direct teaching of young people, and a growing amount of facilitation, advocacy and case management, someone with this background could fulfil the role.

The service briefs

There was evidence that services had developed rapidly over the past few years (mostly during the 1990s); lessons had been learnt about the most effective use of time and, more importantly, initial groundwork in training others had resulted in the specialist team members being freed to engage in further developmental activity – this was particularly exciting, showing a dynamic and maturing system. It should be remembered that the work being done by the teams was completely innovative and the team managers and members had little guidance from senior officers, other than in general management terms or offering 'moral support' as the latter had no experience of practice to share. It is unsurprising that the managers of a few of the specialist services were finding that they were beginning to be involved in a considerable degree of consultancy. It is critically important that wheels are not reinvented – young people looked-after cannot wait that long.

The documentation had developed; the manager of the services which had, perhaps, the most 'mature' documentation admitted that what was presented in 1996 was a long way along the line of drafts since the originals. The most recent version of the general description of the service started with 'entitlements' (to equal opportunities for learning and to the professional collaboration practice that is implied by corporate parenting); thus the fact that services were, quintessentially, ensuring these entitlements was brought to the fore. As resourcing problems were in the background of all the authorities – which is no different from the position nationally – this starting point is judicious: it dispels any remarks that the work of the service is in any way a 'luxury' or something additional that can be disposed of. It is, rather, a means of access. The statement regarding entitlement was followed by one giving the rationale for the service. Again, this was interesting in that it referred to other policy existing in the authority (and, indeed, statutory) – that pupils should be educated alongside their peers in mainstream schools; to the legal position and national reports (the Children Act, the Utting Report and the Staffordshire enquiry); the current education context of market forces and concerns about exclusions; as well as what is now well-known about the difficulties surrounding the education of looked-after children. The rationale thus 'spoke to' other policy-makers and providers within the authority; this is important. It must be remembered that looked-after children represent a tiny minority of the school-aged population. Many people – those who are casting their vote for local government as well as those making decisions within it – are ignorant about the care system and what 'looked-after' status implies. It is, thus, easy to ignore and pass over the problem, or to fail to see how concerted action is needed to address it.

The principal aims of the different services were similar, although with different emphases. Some examples are given below.

- To ensure that children and young people supported by the social services department have access to the best educational opportunities.
- To ensure that, if possible, children and young people 'looked after' by the social services department are maintained in education provision within the authority.
- To monitor, promote and safeguard the education interests of all young people looked after by the local authority or who are known to the social services department
- To facilitate the best and most appropriate education, by minimising educational disadvantage and ensuring that education is seen as a priority in planning for young people being looked after.

In most cases, the overall aim was followed by strategic aims or a list of ways in which the service could assist, or a list of what was available. As the rest of this chapter will be describing the work of the services in greater detail, only two examples of these lists will be given here.

Example 1

What does the Service provide?

- A Head of Service with the strategic brief of ensuring education is given a high priority within all social work initiatives
- Two co-ordinators providing support and advice to all area teams. Their task will be to ensure that the Service responds to the needs of the locality
- A Head of Secure Education to co-ordinate the programmes within the authority's secure units
- A named Support Teacher in each Area team and children's home
- A guaranteed consultancy service for children's homes and social services personnel
- A guaranteed support service for children in secure accommodation and in children's homes
- A needs-led referral service for children in critical need (criteria provided)
- An advice service for children on the threshold of critical need or in families suffering stress (criteria provided)

Example 2

How can we help?

- provision of in-school support
- complementary education packages
- close liaison with the education department
- advice, help and information for all carers
- working with community assessment panels
- advice and help with statements of special educational need
- staff development on education issues
- work experience placements for young people
- college and higher education contacts
- careers, employment seminars with local/national businesses.

As with similar documentation, contact names and addresses were given and there were different leaflets for different audiences (for example, social workers, parents).

Users of the services

Prioritisation

Resources generally dictated who used the services. As services had developed, all had found that they had a greater number of referrals than they were able to cope with; thus criteria for support had to be designed. The group of young people who became eligible for support was, thus, socially constructed. In some cases, young people had to be looked-after; in others, support (in some form) could be extended to children 'in need' in the terms of the Children Act. One interviewee observed that in his authority, 'kids get a better deal if they are accommodated because they get access to the education service'. There was a relentless tension between the desire to do preventative work and the necessity to engage in crisis management, both within teams as a whole and within individual workers' case loads. One team member commented: 'We get end-of-liners when social workers are desperate'; he wondered if it would not be more effective, in the long-term, to do more preventative work. However, with their present level of resources, that would entail sacrificing some of the work which they were doing with the most difficult young people. One social services senior manager observed that the 'end-of-liners' were 'the group who drop out the bottom', who had 'slipped through the net', having failed at the pupil referral unit. Of these young people he said:

> 'They are used like a clipboard: "put the kid on and leave him" and that's the problem solved. They just get a few sessions of home tuition a week.'

Another particularly problematic group were perceived to be those 'with fickle parents' who took them in and out of care: 'They say they're brilliant and take them out of care and then can't cope and put them back into care again'. In one authority there was a particularly rapid turnover of cases such as these: clearly, there are implications here in terms of stable work with the young person if the education support service only works with those who are actually looked-after.

All teams spoke of how they had to prioritise and constantly adjust their work: for example, a priority might be where the foster placement would be rapidly lost unless the child was returned to school. One authority prioritised those children who were in danger of being looked-after, then it supported those in foster care and, finally, those in residential care. This is counter to the position in other authorities, especially those just starting up a service (see chapter two), where the principal concern (perhaps for political reasons) was the situation obtaining in residential care where the most 'difficult' ('socially deviant') young people were placed. In another authority, service team members went to a Family Panel where the cases of families whose child was out of control but not yet looked-after were discussed; team members considered their educational problems and the way in which these related to the domestic stresses.

One senior authority officer remarked, in fact, that admirable though he considered the service in his authority, he yet felt concerned that the root problem of disaffection was not being tackled; others considered that if more preventative work had been done with young people, or other systems had been more responsive, they would not have had substantial periods out of school anyway and thus would not have had to be reintegrated. The situation is complex and there are no easy answers. There was encouraging evidence that some of the services were making a very real difference to practice and decision-making in the authority and were, indeed, eliminating problems.

Cases where the services felt unable to work

A number of practitioners referred to cases from which they had had to withdraw because the young person just refused to co-operate and they could not justify expending resources on him/her while the time and energy would be more profitably focused elsewhere. A manager said:

> 'If we had a referral and we'd had the young person before and it hadn't worked and they'd then had home tuition and it hadn't worked and they'd tried school and ditto, and the young person wasn't prepared to co-operate, then we might say "we can't do this – there's no useful work that we could do". We'd say to re-refer when the young person was more co-operative. This would be unusual because young people normally work with us.'

Another team member explained: 'We've a waiting list and if you can't achieve anything then you sometimes have to cut your losses and work with someone else'. This may be a sad fact of life but the way it is managed is important. First, best practice suggested that it was possible for the group of 'non-co-operators' to change monthly – that is, young people were going through short periods where they were not co-operating but they were not totally opting out of the system. One authority collected data on the profile of non-attenders and non-co-operators and evaluated them in terms of the movement represented – there was cause for concern where it was static. Second, a few young people may need to be left out of education for some time while they sort out other problems in their lives but they need to be able to return and pick up the support later. There is considerable anecdotal evidence that young people who have been in the care system often want to return to education after the turbulent adolescent years have past; the ways in which systems can provide for this – after they have officially left care – were not explored in this research project, which was focusing on young people of statutory school age. Nevertheless, the need for this issue to be addressed was highlighted by the data collected in the present research.

Some young people, on account of their previous lifestyle simply did not 'fit' the education system. For example, an officer described the following case.

> 'At the moment we've lots children with no school. For example, one girl has had a nomadic lifestyle. We've tried to get her settled in a place but reckon that, with her, "success" is knowing where she is for a couple of nights a week. But are we failing her? She is very resistant to one-to-one. The service fixed up a place at [the PRU] but it didn't work. We couldn't offer her anything attractive to replace her former lifestyle. She's only 14 and has rejected anything formal. She's had hours of support – it's not for want of trying.'

Types of school involved

Some teams were able to support young people in all types of school (special as well as mainstream and, in some cases, in out-authority residential). One team did not support in special schools because of resource limitations; it was considered that these schools should, by their very nature, have adequate specialist staff to meet the pupils' needs (though there was research evidence that this was not, in fact, the case – see chapter six).

Most teams focused on adolescents, though some did work with pupils of primary school age and all observed that they were increasingly being directed to pupils of younger ages, and in one case mentioned, to the early years' phase. This pattern is reflected in national figures which, though sometimes hard to interpret with any accuracy, suggest that an increasing number of pupils in key stages one and two are being excluded.

Regardless of their formal referral criteria and brief, all teams were valued and noted for the way in which they were immediately responsive to enquiries and generous with their advice. Carers, in particular, spoke warmly of the way in which they could just phone up the team's base for a word of advice or reassurance – maybe for something as trivial as the name of a contact. In many cases, this response and the flexibility and accessibility of the team were sharply contrasted with interviewees' experiences of the education department where problems of delay, bureaucracy and access to information were common. The research resources were insufficient to check out all the tales told and so injustices may have been done; nonetheless, perceptions are important and the data were certainly common through all the case study authorities. To a certain extent this finding is unsurprising. The teams were positioned between social services and education departments and were innovative; they thus created their own rules and *modus operandi* and, though there were clear lines of accountability, most practitioners felt that they were working for the child. Indeed, one of their perceived strengths was that they could challenge fellow professionals: they could ask schools why they had not followed exclusion procedures; they could badger education departments about delays in finding school places; they could question social services about the appropriateness of care placements. In sum, the advocacy role was first and foremost even if it did also involve, in its mature form, collaborating with, rather than confronting, other agencies.

As well as the young people, users included social service officers, teachers and carers. Incidents reported in chapter five, for example, show how carers were very often able to take responsibility for supporting children once they knew what to do and how to go about it. The support services observed that an intervention with foster parents – to change behaviour or strategies, for example – could negate the need for a direct intervention with the young person. This is important; as has been observed before, these young people so often have a bewildering number of adults intervening in their lives, particularly those in residential care where increasingly units offer specialist, short-term interventions after which the young people move on elsewhere. Forming relationships rapidly is a demanding social skill for anyone; it is often relentlessly required of those very young people who have not been in a favourable position to make trusting relationships.

Service managers made the point that the actual number of young people looked-after with whom the service was working at any one time gave a distorted picture as, if the service had been effective in sensitising systems, then there would be many other young people who would be influenced tangentially and via other agents. One manager said: 'There are lots achieving and not supported by the service because their social workers have been re-educated'. Furthermore, the throughput in the course of a year could be many more than those on the books at any one time. Contracts were rarely open-ended and, although durations could range from two weeks to two years, there were always specific aims and objectives, with regular review and evaluation (essentially, the processes promoted in the Code of Practice). The nature of the support was in this respect dissimilar to that allocated to pupils with statements of special educational needs where a child with a visual impairment, for example, might need support for a number of years. The support was given in order to stabilise situations, assist integration and show others how to maintain inclusion.

The characteristics of the young people

Behavioural difficulties

The young people were, needless to say, as varied as any group of young people might be in terms of their preferences and individual characteristics. However, those involved with the education support services tended to present difficult behaviour. As is discussed elsewhere, those who were stable and progressing unproblematically tended not to benefit from additional support because the prime aim, in practice, of the services was to maintain education so that care plans could be fulfilled. The broad aim, presented above, of ensuring the 'best' educational opportunities for looked-after children was not, in practice, being achieved as yet, largely because of resource issues rather than lack of awareness of need or desire to address it; this will be considered in chapter seven. The young people were generally said to need a lot of personal attention – something which, clearly, schools found it hard to provide and which made staying out of schools and thus securing the attention of an adult or adults during the day, attractive to young people. One residential manager observed that 'they love having the staff here round them all day'; another that 'it's easier staying at home and causing havoc'. A further commented:

> 'It used to be that they didn't have uniform or kit or that teachers were too nice to them. Now it's because they're disruptive and gain attention by acting out because they're so lacking in confidence.'

A social worker said:

> 'They see themselves as worthless. If you're going to be bad you might as well go the whole hog ... School should be a positive experience to help them mature ... Schools must look beyond that disruptive behaviour and find something positive to work on.'

This comment relates to what some saw as the fundamental issue which the education support services should address, as will be discussed below.

Previous educational histories

Mostly, the young people had had negative educational experiences – compounding the negative social and personal experiences in their lives. Interviewees spoke of young people who had had multiple breakdowns of school places and had been excluded from mainstream, day special, authority residential special and out-authority residential special schools – following which they were returned to their home area for social services to make provision for. A strategy employed by one residential unit manager was to get the child's key worker to go through the child's file to find some evidence of educational success or some time when they were happy in, and positive about, school: 'for example, go back to the infant school and seek out the teacher and talk about the kid – and then remind the young person of this'.

School difficulties

The reasons for not fitting in at school were extremely variable. All flowed, fundamentally, from the young people's previous experiences out of school: case after case was told of dire neglect or abuse. Some clashed with the authority figure of the teacher; some clashed with their peers and were subject to, or the perpetrators of, bullying. One residential carer remarked that some simply found it hard to concentrate and meet the social/academic demands: 'they take direction OK because we're pretty tight with them here'.

Yet another group refused school not because they had difficulties there or disliked it but because they were concerned about the home situation. A child was understandably reluctant to stay in school if s/he felt that family members might 'disappear' during the day and not be there when s/he returned. A case was told of a seven-year old girl who refused to go to school as she was worried what would happen to her mother, whom she had seen being the target of her father's violence and whom she felt that she ought to protect. Another 5/6 year old was tearful at school, having recently come into foster care, because he wanted his 'real mum and dad'. A common complaint of social workers and carers was that some teachers assumed that all their pupils came from stable, middle-class homes; they seemed to have no awareness of the intolerable traumas that some of their pupils were going through and the stresses which would tax an adult, let alone a child.

Learning difficulties

Although many of the young people with whom the education support services were working had learning difficulties, there were cases of young people hiding their abilities and, equally, cases where there had been inappropriate placements in special schools. Despite the fact that all interviewees were positively disposed to education, belief in the young people's academic success was uncommon, apart from in particularly positive homes and with members of the education support service. A head of unit said:

> 'And at the end of the day, just getting the kids to school is an achievement. But I think the book closes not so far away from that. We don't have any high flyers.'

But an experienced foster carer questioned whether lack of learning was on account of actual learning difficulties:

> 'I get some kids at 14/15 and they can't read or write. School has been happy so long as they sit at the back and behave. What a waste! Why no earlier intervention? They're quite intelligent kids and will converse well ... Most have been the class clown because this is easier than getting the work done ... They have lots of friends rather than get stuck in and not have so many friends ... it depends a lot on the school.'

An education support service teacher cited the case of a boy who had been excluded from 13 schools yet got five or six GCSEs because at the school he finally settled in at key stage four 'the staff treated him with respect and worked with his success'.

In some cases, schools' 'normal' expectations of the young people were too high given the amount of schooling that the latter had missed.

'Culture'

A number of young people looked-after came from areas where there had been a high level of unemployment for several generations – the demotivating and depressing effect of this on pupils' attitudes to school has been well-documented elsewhere. But, again, this 'universal' fact has the potential to have a disproportionate effect on young people who feel personally worthless for family reasons (through neglect, abuse of whatever) and do not view school as a place offering positive experiences – over and above the 'external' reasons – the state of the local economy, for example. A foster carer said:

> 'I've got this theory that having seen these different kids come through, that there is such a low esteem attached to education in some areas ... You take the high rise – I've got one of those now. She goes to school but she sees no reason to go to school. She's no reason to co-operate when she gets to school but that's because her parents were like that and she's been brought up to think that way ... So you can't change attitudes.'

This foster carer had, in fact, 'changed attitudes' by working on the girl's liking of cooking and suggesting catering and hotel work for which she pointed out that the girl would need English and maths GCSE – 'she's turned over a new leaf'. The way she worked – starting with the girl's strengths and interests – is relevant to the 'core problem' discussed below.

The perceptions of the young people

The following comments were made by looked-after pupils to the NFER researcher. They need no gloss as each implicitly, vividly and succinctly challenges various aspects of school life.

- [Schools could] 'Take more time out to see what's up with them, what's upset them and, if they're not there, ask them what's up.'
  (13 year old)

- 'I felt it was frustrating having to start over and over again, and you have to start one level of work then go to another school and start another level ... There were a lot of people you had to get to know.'
  (12 year old)

- 'Before I met X [the education support service teacher] I just thought to myself, "I'm no good in school, I've got nowt to go to school for, I just hate it" ... When I started seeing X I started listening to what he had to say so then after that I started to take advice off X and then I started changing and started liking school.' *(15 year old)*

- When asked if he 'lashed out' because teachers 'shouted at him' rather than talked to him, one boy, in care since he was four and having had five placements, said: 'Well, I'd rather be talked to but then in some case the other pupils will be thinking, "well, he gets the good treatment and we get the hard treatment".' *(12 year old)*

- 'I was in care when I went to secondary school. The friends I did have when I went up there I didn't have when I went into care because their mums had told them to keep away from me being in the care unit. So I lost most of my friends and because I lost most of my friends I caused more and more trouble ... It's the numbers in school – I don't like to be crowded. If I'm stuck on something and I need a teacher and the teacher is busy with someone else then I get ratty because I think I'm thick and then I take it out on my friends and stuff. So it's best to keep me away ... Here there's always someone to help you ... it's a lot friendlier ... they're like your best friends ... it's brilliant – they teach you more than at school ... always someone there ... get through it quicker ... they've done loads for me.' *(15 year old)*

The fundamental issues to be addressed

All the research in the area points out the tasks to be done. However, it was noticeable that all the services worked with a similar ideology: they were committed to the young people's success and believed that they could achieve this given the right support at the right time. The vast majority of those interviewed were extremely positive and enthusiastic people as regards their work and, implicitly or explicitly, worked on the 'small steps' principle common in special education. Briefly, this assumes small, manageable, viable and regularly reviewed targets, and works on the model of facilitating and celebrating achievement and success in order to progress to the next challenge.

One service manager discounted many of the 'problems' attributed to this area of work as 'excuses'. He identified the core problems as follows:

- lack of will: the excuse of members and senior management here was that they could not do it because of the resource implications
- social workers' training: the focus was on difficulties and problems rather than potential and strengths; this permeated all practice and affected expectations
- the social work system: all assessment forms tended to bring out the negative. There was a need to build on strengths to overcome this and promote success; social workers needed to realise that 'success' was the 'therapy' on which they were all so keen; there was undue emphasis on the 'myth' of specialist provision.

What, then, was the strategy to overcome these problems? He said that it was vital to ask what the young people can or could do, then ask how to get them to do this, and then ask what they needed to do it (the resource question). This was, he pointed out, counter to the normal approach of 'can't, won't so remove' or saying that the child can't cope in school because there were inadequate resources. The service which he had built up 'challenges all working with looked-after children to tell something positive about the young person'; this approach had permeated standard practice within the social services department as regards assessment and provision. This manager had arrived at this approach through first-hand practical experience of working with some extremely difficult young people. It had been assumed that they would not, or could not, maintain a place in mainstream school but, after a change of strategy in their management, this was proved to be a false assumption.

Another manager said:

> 'The education support service is about changing attitudes and perceptions. We must work to encourage social services and residential care home staff to become more positive about the role of schools. With schools, we have to offer workable strategies for support and communication.'

Summary

- Responsibility for funding and management of discrete education support services for looked-after children fell to either social services or education departments, or was shared; the larger and more experienced services were located within social services departments;

- different local contexts determined particular service arrangements, particularly as regards the users of the service and referral procedures;

- staff in specialised support services came from a wide range of backgrounds; background was less important than interpersonal skills such as the ability to work with a range of adults and the ability to move with ease between social services and education environments;

- policies, procedures and documentation in those authorities which had dedicated support education services for looked-after children had undergone rapid evolution and there is a wealth of experience on which newer services can draw;

- some documents stressed that service provision was merely ensuring young people's entitlement to education;

- resources generally dictated who used the services; all services were inundated with referrals and had more requests for help than support available;

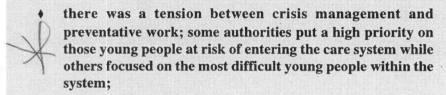

- there was a tension between crisis management and preventative work; some authorities put a high priority on those young people at risk of entering the care system while others focused on the most difficult young people within the system;

- the planning of service provision was particularly difficult where children were moved in and out of the care system; in all cases teams had to work flexibly;

- service providers had to acknowledge that there might be a small minority of looked-after young people who refused any educational intervention at any one time; the aim was that this group should be fluid so that any one young person was not without education for any length of time;

- most services focused on adolescents although it was widely reported that the number of referrals regarding children of primary school age was increasing;

- service providers were keen to assist schools and carers in supporting young people who were looked-after and did not offer long-term support to any individual young person;

- users particularly valued services' responsiveness and accessibility;

- many young people receiving support presented behavioural or learning difficulties, generally on account of personal experiences including previous neglect of education;

- young people were able to give an insight into the educational difficulties generated by their being looked-after;

- service staff considered that the key to successful provision was a belief in the young person's capacity for a positive educational career, and a determination to bring this about.

CHAPTER 4
THE EDUCATION SUPPORT SERVICES
– PRACTICE

This chapter will describe the work of the services and discuss the many activities in which staff engaged.

Mediation

All services perceived themselves, and were perceived, as a bridging facility, spanning the divide between the education and the social services departments. However much inter-agency collaboration is talked about, the fact remains that it is extremely difficult and actual joint working is rare (the most positive examples being in early years' work). The fact that the services 'had a foot in both camps' and provided an objective service focused on the immediate needs of the child, was widely acknowledged to be a critical feature, justifying the discrete service and countering arguments that support could be provided by existing agencies. The 'objectivity' was widely referred to. It was the perception of one interviewee that statutory services tended to protect their own – excuses were made for inaction, for example – and in some cases, they 'set up cushy relationships with schools that are best for their colleagues rather than the children'. The education support services never criticised colleagues – though they might point out their statutory obligations – but were able to cut through the micro-politics, as it were. In all authorities, the services were praised for the following:

- mediating schools' views to social services

- challenging social services a) to follow child protection procedures – (where schools were concerned about children whom social services did not seem to be investigating); and b) about the wisdom of proposed care placements – where these would disrupt educational placements

- challenging schools a) to follow statutory exclusion procedures (where they were excluding unadvisedly); and b) regarding admissions and available places – where carers and social workers had been told that the school was full

- challenging local education authorities to provide alternative education for excluded pupils.

A team leader said: 'It is about maximising the number of children I can help by working with other people'. Another commented that it was 'telling the LEA to do its bit – the [education support service] is *extra* and shouldn't replace normal responsibilities'.

Support service workers were in a prime position by virtue of their unique position:

- they could have an overview of the case

- they were not associated with the 'root' of the problem (as carers sometimes were)

- they were not at the centre of the problem (as were teachers who were having to control difficult pupils in the classroom)

- they had the necessary technical knowledge (for example, about exclusions and child protection)

- they were viewed as fellow professionals by colleagues in both social services and education departments and in schools

- they had expertise and experience in dealing with children who were looked-after (schools, as pointed out elsewhere, may have one on roll infrequently)

- they were regarded by foster parents and carers as more accessible and friendly than teachers at school

- they were experienced at, and generally comfortable with, working with all levels of management.

As one social services manager said: 'They know the right buttons to press – they enable us to access education for our children'; while a carer remarked: 'She [the service teacher] really makes a difference – she makes things happen – she oils the wheels between social services and education'.

Service staff could very often reduce time scales and delay by knowing immediately the right person to go to or the most effective procedure to follow; they could work round bureaucratic processes. This was very important, given the adverse effect on care plans of young people being out of school, for example.

Informing

Informing is, clearly, linked to mediation although it does carry a different aspect. In mediation activities, the support service workers actually did the mediation – they went along to the school with the carers, for example, attended the governors' meeting, went to multi-disciplinary panels. In informing activities, they made it easier for colleagues to work with young people and communicated information that would enhance their working practices.

General issues about information exchange

In the words of one interviewee, 'information can be a powerful commodity'; all the service managers were concerned to collect and communicate data that increased understanding of how to work with looked-after children and, moreover, to use data rather than just collect them. Information technology was perceived as a useful tool for monitoring and evaluation. The lack of data has been something highlighted by all previous research; comparisons about educational placements and attainments of looked-after young people are simply not yet possible because the statistics are not yet available. However, the position was changing in all the case study authorities: data were being kept systematically and were, moreover, being increasingly used to inform policy and practice. In particular, systems had to be capable of accommodating early intervention – that is, they had both to trigger appropriate responses and yield the data sufficiently frequently; the example was given of data about unauthorised absences.

On an individual basis, it was a matter not only of giving and eliciting initial information but of maintaining the communication. As one social worker said: 'Sometimes it's just a matter of putting a note in your diary to ring school X'.

What information was available

There were, however, still 'files being lost in the system' and carers said that information on admission about a child's education was generally thin unless 'the child has been around for a long time – in which case you get worried anyway!' or the education support service had previously worked with the child. This again reinforces the point made elsewhere that the impact of what education support services did, or could do, was potentially much greater than the sum of the young people with whom they were actively working. Although examination of files on young people with whom the services were working showed that information was kept in an exemplary fashion in the majority of cases, the collation of data on the education of all looked-after children as a group is still in its early stages. Again, the Department of Health materials may help here.

Emergency admissions rarely had adequate educational histories – most were cases of abuse or neglect anyway where the parents would not have been likely to provide these data. Another common perception was that the information given was often inaccurate. One interviewee said: 'a lot of reports do get over-sensationalised in order to get a placement – which is sad, really', while others complained about the reverse situation – that too rosy a picture was painted of the child. This seemed to apply particularly to foster carers – perhaps residential staff were aware that they would be receiving the 'hardest' of cases. Clearly, in view of the shortage of foster placements, it is unsurprising that social workers do not accentuate the problems. However, no foster parents interviewed intimated that they would have refused the placement; rather they considered that it would have been more helpful, in terms of planning strategies, were they in receipt of as much information as possible. 'They say she's got a school place but not that she doesn't go.'

All those working with young people looked-after said that they needed relevant information in order to work with the child (they had to know the 'history' of their difficulties), to support them in their education careers and, in a few cases, to protect staff and other pupils (in cases where the young person had a history of violence or perpetration of abuse, for example). A foster carer said:

> 'There's got to be strict recording of school, what he likes doing, behaviour, educational needs, so you can start talking about these needs ... at college you can say that course involves maths and his records show that he's had problems with maths. Or that one needs a bus ride and he can't cope ... All educational developments ought to be on file ... otherwise you can go through five social workers to find the rest of the case notes ... I could tell you what school he went to but not how he performed or what problems he had ... all I know about him is the one school he went to.'

A social services team manager spoke at length about the problem of data collection. Clearly, the comments were related to his particular authority; in some of the other case study authorities, practice in residential care was more advanced.

'Even if a child has been in our care for some time, we don't get to know educational information such as educational standards and expectations. It's much easier for fostered children – you know if they're being stretched or allowed to flounder ... if the child is in residential and accommodated, the parent may offer to go to school and this cuts you off from the information. Foster carers will share things with you fully – they'll say to the child 'go and show X your reading book or what you've just achieved'. ... You don't get that for an accommodated child ... We know very little about statements. For example, we had a girl who had been in an education unit attached to a residential children's home, then went into 52 week placement out-authority, then got excluded and is now in a school in [adjacent authority]. We've known her from the age of nine but it has only just emerged that she had a statement at seven following a psychiatric assessment, and was a day pupil at a hospital school (child psychiatric unit). We knew none of this; it's probably in a file in the education department but we don't have parental responsibility so can't access this.'

Educational statistics about looked-after children as a group

As was seen in chapter two and established in previous research, there is a dearth of data about the educational placements, careers and attainment of looked-after young people. Data that are widely quoted have frail foundations, being based on small samples and on 'snapshots'. However, the case study authorities were in the forefront of ameliorating this situation. In some cases, 'snapshots' – such as that taken by Ofsted/SSI (1995) – had alerted officers and members to incipient problems, especially in residential care.

An Information Digest giving figures for a nine-month period following the reorganisation of one of the support services provided data on clients by social service area, gender, age, educational placement, key stage, attendance, statement of special educational needs, care placement, legal status; a more detailed breakdown was undertaken for those in residential care. The analysis of these data allowed the team to identify areas of development: for example, as well as the problem of minimal educational provision for young people in residential care, it appeared that there was an increasing problem at transfer from primary to secondary school.

In another authority, the service manager examined the academic end of key stage achievements of young people looked-after. Although significantly below the national average for the age cohort (52 per cent five GCSE as against 86 per cent; 4 per cent gaining five or more GCSE grades A-C, as against 17 per cent) and giving no cause for complacency, the figures nevertheless showed that a proportion of the relevant population in the authority did pass. Furthermore, the staying-on rate and placement in further education was no different from that of mainstream (74 per cent of the authority's young people and 72 per cent of all young people nationally – and an estimated 35 per cent of looked-after children nationally). Elsewhere, an analysis of data showed that the attendance patterns of looked-after young people in some areas could be better than those of other pupils in inner-city areas of the same authority. Clearly, trans-authority comparisons are unviable at the moment as snapshots are taken at different times of the year and they operate on different calculations of the looked-after population. However, the important thing is that they are being collected and being used to allocate resources and inform policy and practice.

Informing other officers

Several teams prepared digests of documentation relating to educational legislation (for example, DFE circular 10/94 on exclusions, or the Code of Practice) for social services managers, assisting them to answer the question 'What implications does this have for us?' Social services managers spoke of the volumes of material that arrived on their desks to read and greatly valued having the team's help in filtering some of it so that they could then pass it on to their own social services team members as appropriate, as well as being accurately informed at a managerial level. Similar work was done for teachers – for example, about the technicalities of what being looked-after meant, or the implications of the Children Act.

Most of the services had structured systems of support for professional colleagues such as 'help' telephone lines, contact people in each area office, or local 'surgeries' or 'advice shops' where a member of staff would be on tap to answer any queries or give on-the-spot advice to social workers or anyone who cared to call in. All this was greatly valued, not only for the quality of the advice, but for the ready and immediate access to it – reference was made to this time and time again.

Informing carers

Support teachers were able to inform carers about educational achievement and interpret the National Curriculum, for example. An interviewee spoke of how easy it is to assume that foster carers will understand school reports. She told the story of how, as she explained the differences between National Curriculum assessment levels, a foster parent said: 'Just tell me, is it a bicycle or a bollocking?' Other carers spoke of how the child's records would say that s/he was doing well at school but, on closer scrutiny by the support workers, they would discover that the child was, in reality, attaining at a low level. They also said that support service workers 'would know what to look for and what questions to ask' – for example, how homework diaries were, or should be, used; what special educational needs support was available.

Carers were also interested in information about the child's social development at school – for example, if they were able to get on in small or large groups, if they could cope in unstructured time such as the lunch-hour; if they were isolates or lacking in confidence; this would inform work done at home.

Informing schools and education providers

A lot of the work of the services involved raising the awareness of schools as to the experience of being looked-after, helping teachers to understand why pupils were presenting with unacceptable behaviour and, most importantly, informing them of strategies that had proved effective with the young person concerned. After this initial 'informing', service staff had to ensure that communication channels were kept open. Where practice was embryonic in schools or residential units, the support teachers often did this informing themselves, particularly where they were working intensively with a young person in school. Elsewhere, services had done a lot to ensure that other agents were aware of what relevant information ought to be passed on. The head of a pupil referral unit said not unreasonably:

> 'We have interesting debates with the [education support service] and care workers regarding sharing information. For example, if the kids come into the residential children's home drunk, smash the place up, the police are called in, they spend the night in the cell, get no sleep and then are sent off to the PRU in the morning, we need to know. Some social workers say it's not our business but it affects what we do with them. Otherwise, we don't need to know why they're in care etc. unless it impinges on our staff (for example, if a girl has been sexually abused or a boy is particularly violent).'

The final comment in the above quotation is important. A member of staff in a school visited during the research made the comment that they did not have information about what went on in the lives of pupils who were looked-after; there was a thin line between what was relevant information and what was unjustified intrusion. Generally, education support service staff acted on the 'need to know' principle and were experienced judges of what information was relevant and purposeful. Information was given where it would help teachers to respond to the young person: for example, one boy 'lived in a fantasy world' but this would not be apparent unless teachers were told that he was not reporting actual events.

Very obviously, support services also did a vast amount of work informing professional decision-makers about the whole issue of the education of looked-after children and the impact of education on care work. The head of the pupil referral unit cited above said:

> 'X [head of service] has put in lot of work to get education put back on the agenda ... Care workers were not bothered where kids were so long as they weren't around the children's home ... Social workers were thinking that there were priorities higher than education ... Schools were saying 'go away, we don't want you'. ... It's slow, hard work but it's getting through that you can't make decisions that are OK in social work terms but disrupt education.'

Informing looked-after young people

Finally, team members were able to inform young people. It was generally observed that, before intervention, many young people looked-after had no ideas about careers or post-16 options. The work of teams in broadening their horizons and enabling them to think of more challenging paths to take on leaving school was very important. One authority arranged careers evenings, where local businesses and colleges would come along to talk with young people. It should be pointed out that the informing was usually complemented by practical help in securing placements – the service staff would, for example, go along to college with a young person and support them through the process of application (though in some cases this function was fulfilled by carers). It may be asked why this activity was necessary: after all, there are careers services and information about post-16 options is readily available to all young people. The answer is the same as that given before: in order to ensure equality of opportunity there has to be positive discrimination. Young people looked-after, particularly those with a poor school attendance record, may simply have missed out on careers advice and guidance, or they may have had such a poor opinion of themselves that they discounted anything but the most mundane job. The core message was the same: in order to repair fragmentation, additional action may have to be taken. Most young people, after all, receive firm support from family members at times of transition. Looked-after young people are having to make transition plans without this support and, furthermore, at a time when they are leaving care and having to face the prospects of independent living – something which is daunting to 16 year olds who have come from well-organised families providing a sound role model of competence.

Meetings and reviews

In most cases, the education support services had a policy of attendance at meetings. Managers considered that this was essential to ensure that education was put on the agenda in as many forums as possible – and kept there. The maintenance function was as critical as the initial awareness-raising. However, there was a feeling among some team members that the position should be carefully monitored; in some cases they felt that meetings were not a good use of their time, once they had, for example, determined how other agencies functioned, which might be better spent working directly with clients. A lot depended, of course, on the purpose and the management of the meeting.

The question of review meetings was often raised. In one authority, the team was committed to attending all 72 hour reviews (the initial planning meeting which has, by law, to be held after reception into care). This was to ensure that education was 'upfront' and was highly valued by some practitioners. However, others questioned whether this was a waste of staff time, particularly where the meetings would cover many other issues not directly related to education and where there were a lot of such meetings – in a short-term assessment unit for example. Staff commonly attended three and six monthly review meetings – whether or not schools were or should be involved in these is discussed in chapter six.

The necessity of education support service staff attending reviews was determined to a certain extent by the awareness of whoever was chairing the review. A review manager spoke of how it was easy for all the time to be spent in a review on a matter of higher priority; education could be 'lost' in this way – although there were specific questions on the relevant review form – or salient issues could be raised almost by chance. In one review that she had recently conducted the young person was at the end of key stage three. When the review manager asked who had discussed the girl's option choices with her, 'both the key worker and the social worker' looked blank: no one had, in fact, done this. The review manager said that it was only by chance that she 'had asked the question'.

Managing information

One of the tasks that the managers of education support services took on was that of establishing and maintaining the effective management of information about looked-after children. This was on two levels: the individual and the collective.

As regards the individual level, services were moving towards standardised forms seeking information about clients initially (for referral purposes) and while working with the case (for purposes of monitoring, review and evaluation); and for collating data about individual looked-after children's educational careers, whether or not they were active clients of the service. The latter could often be dispersed among a number of files, individual carers and social workers. As stated in chapter two, many authorities nationally were committed to the Department of Health's Looking After Children documentation (see Dartington Social Research Unit, 1995; Corrick *et al.*, 1995; Jackson and Kilroe, 1995) and were beginning to embed this into working practices; it had focused social workers' attention routinely on education and reinforced the work of support services.

At the collective service level, service managers were regularly collecting data about the placement and attendance of looked-after children; this was so that monitoring could take place and there be early intervention if 'warning signs' were picked up. They were also in dialogue with relevant colleagues in the authority regarding the use of authority-wide data collection and management information systems. In the majority of cases there were severe but not intractable problems regarding the incompatibility or insufficiency of both hardware and software. Although agencies 'shared' clients, they had no means of sharing information, other than on a manual basis. This was for both technical and conceptual reasons. Technically, both the means of collection and the methods of processing data did not allow for easy communication across departments and agencies; conceptually, education departments did not regard looked-after children as a discrete category while social services departments did not regard looked-after children with special educational needs as a discrete category. Thus, hypothetically, several support services (from social services and from education) could be working with a pupil without any collaboration. It was members of the education support services who picked up these anomalies on an individual case base; the challenge, however, was to collect and communicate data systematically and routinely. Although some of the case study authorities had moved a long way along the road, none yet considered that the problem was solved; there was a certain degree of frustration in some areas on account of lack of resources to amend systems.

Services also acted as 'information agencies'. For example, they were often valued for their knowledge of resources available locally; interestingly, a number of carers asked for resource handbooks, saying that it was good luck rather than good management if they were directed to the right place. Support service workers often had a wider knowledge than did social workers, especially in areas where there was a rapid turn-over of staff with new staff unfamiliar with local provision arriving regularly.

Case loads

What team members actually did depended entirely on their particular case load. Case loads themselves varied in number. There was consensus among managers that set numbers of cases could not be allocated to staff as the intensity of the intervention varied. In some cases, where integration was being arranged, involvement could be extremely intensive (see below); elsewhere it might entail a regular session with a pupil each week; in other cases it might only be as required or to keep a watchful eye on the case. As interventions were invariably task-related rather than 'linear', much depended on the young person's response, the way that significant adults in the environment responded (for example, a primary aged child's class teacher) or what was happening in the care placement. Most teams held regular meetings at which existing case loads were discussed and new referrals considered. The latter were slotted in to members of the team who had space and/or seemed to be suited, in terms of particular skills, personality or experiences, to the needs of the young person.

One worker sketched a reasonably typical day as follows:

visit *residential children's home*	check education support plans work informally with residential staff attend staff meeting
visit *school*	provide in-class support spend time with the child
	meet with staff to review progress, resolve difficulties
visit *council offices*	attend policy meeting

On another day, there might be visits to foster parents or a formal review.

Induction programmes

One of the authorities had a policy of putting in place an induction programme for all looked-after young people returning to school, transferring or coming from an outside placement. This is described below.

- Records and histories are collected by the support service teacher allocated to the case and the level of the child's work is discussed. Then a school is approached for a place and a (re)entry date negotiated so that the school can prepare for and is prepared for the pupil. The teacher co-ordinates all arrangements and information for that pupil and dates are set for review. The teacher contacts all the mainstream teachers who will teach that child; this is negotiated with the school admissions tutor or the relevant head of year – whoever is handling the case overall. The teacher explains to the mainstream teacher that s/he will be in lessons with the new pupil at first to see how the pupil responds to that lesson and identify difficulties. There is also discussion with the class teacher, who will be the best person to inform the support teacher as to the group dynamics among the peer group and how the new pupil will be received. It is considered imperative that the mainstream teacher trusts the support teacher. The support teacher is essentially making an assessment to see what is needed. S/he will discuss with the mainstream teacher(s) things like the level of literacy required to access worksheets and what differentiated materials are available. S/he will ask to see examples of pupils' work so that the level of expectations can be gauged.

- The end product is a profile of the child's needs at the time; this will include an assessment of the child's responses outside the classroom – for example, one child will fall in with a peer group at lunchtime while another will be totally terrified of the social demands of this. Demands made by registration time and lesson changeover time are considered, together with opportunities for extra-curricular activities.

- The period of observation lasts one or two weeks, depending on the child. It could be followed by full-time support for a month, even a half-term in some cases. In some cases the service buys in sessional workers to support the child. The key thing for the school is that there is discussion about time-limited pieces of work that are directed towards putting the child back on his/her feet in the school.

- There is a review of progress every couple of weeks and the child is involved in the discussion of support needed. Support can be increased or decreased according to how things have gone in the period reviewed. Schools always know what is happening and there is a high degree of trust. All arrangements are recorded. Much of the communication is face-to-face and the support teachers go into staffrooms. The form tutor is usually central – they attend reviews with the head of year. The support teachers are, essentially, doing what mainstream teachers could do but have not the time for.

This practice is, clearly, labour-intensive and costly. However, it ensures as far as is possible that the environment will be set up to facilitate success – rather than failure, as is so often the case. In terms of the longer-term benefits accruing, it is justified. The practice is not common but previous NFER research in the area of special educational needs has found similar work (see Fletcher-Campbell *et al.*, 1992) in relation to the integration of pupils with learning difficulties; again, the intensive work was considered extremely valuable and worthwhile, albeit costly.

Task-related support

The following comment sums up one of the key features of the education support services: 'we are offering teachers the opportunity to meet needs rather than just identify them.' The nature of the support given in the above example was typical of the services as a whole: each was insistent that it was not an alternative to special educational needs support, nor a long-term measure. To refer to the point made in chapter one, the business was facilitating exclusion and inclusion, not actual teaching. However, because the context into which the support was going was one in which there was a shortage of resources generally and, in particular, special needs support, withdrawal sometimes posed a problem. It is worth quoting a senior member of a support service at some length:

> 'The other thing that is quite difficult is putting in the amount of support that ideally there should be, but in reality we can't provide – we haven't enough manpower to do it. And also being asked to do things that are not our responsibility ... We're quite clear that the work that we're doing is to meet a social work objective with education very, very high on the agenda. But we're looking at making sure that the young person has access to his/her rightful education etc. – it's not our job to provide special education for a child who has a statement of special educational need, for instance. Inevitably if you're going to start working with a young person you're going to help them with their education, but you have to be very clear about what the objective of our intervention is – not because Johnny can't read, but because he can't read and therefore he probably exhibits all sort of inappropriate behaviours which may lead to him being excluded, and if he's excluded, he's going to lose his foster placement. It's getting into that that's quite difficult, and once schools get hold of our support, which tends to be of a higher level in terms of time than they're able to get from anywhere else, they're very reluctant to let it go once they've got it and that can be quite difficult – difficult for the teachers to back out.'

In some schools, task-related support involved the sensitive issue of engaging in teacher guidance: there were some instances where teachers were differentiating the work inadequately or their classroom management was such that it gave opportunities for difficult looked-after pupils to display inappropriate behaviour. Elsewhere, pastoral matters were not handled with sufficient sensitivity: there was an incident, for example, where an adolescent girl was drawn into a fight, which had serious consequences, largely because when she sought help, in the knowledge that confrontation was imminent, teachers did not take the request seriously. Clearly, all this guidance had to be given with sensitivity; support teachers were operating in the knowledge that they had to work in the same classrooms and schools again. But the upshot was that in many cases, staff were engaging in staff development with mainstream teachers (much in the same way that happens when special education specialists support a pupil by working with the teacher). This has implications, not only in terms of the training or experience that support teachers should have but also in terms of the potential benefits that accrue to classrooms in which the effective ones are working: although data had not been collected in any systematic way, it was the perception of some support teachers that schools changed tactics and tried new strategies with pupils other than those who were looked-after, simply because they had been introduced to new ways of working by the visiting support teachers.

Some support was given in the classroom. As with support for pupils with special educational needs, the actual method of working varied according to the pupil's needs and preferences. Some young people were said to enjoy having their 'special adult' in the classroom – peers were, apparently, envious of the attention. Others would not countenance being singled out in this way and support teachers would work generally within the classroom, albeit implicitly focusing on the young person whom they were supporting. A deputy head in a school where support teachers were working said: 'They do it so well it doesn't make the child stand out'. A head of year in a school that worked closely with the support service teachers remarked: 'It's important that no one has the opportunity to say to the kid "you can't operate without someone by your side".' A young person looked-after who was interviewed mentioned the dangers of being singled out in any way: 'It starts a lot of arguments and in some cases started fights'. This, in turn, led to the young person being excluded.

Other support was given in withdrawal sessions. Sometimes these might be to review the pupil's work, or their behaviour over the week or in a lesson; sometimes they were used to reward the pupil – going to McDonalds was widely favoured! Individual members of staff were largely free to work in ways which suited them and their clients. At times, the reasons that the child was looked-after rose to the fore inappropriately in school – support staff had to be prepared and sufficiently sensitive to deal with these. The instance was given of a girl who had suffered sexual abuse from her grandfather – he had also videoed the sessions; she was discussing the event with other pupils in her class. Clearly, action needed to be taken here and, in this case, it was the support teacher who did this as she was 'on the spot' as it were.

Arranging packages

With adolescents, teaching service input was often in the form of arranging 'packages' of education, especially where the young people concerned would not be able to tolerate a full week in the mainstream classroom – or would not be tolerated there. These packages might include time in school, on an alternative education project and on work experience, together with some home tuition or sessional work from the education support service; the aim was to offer something which not only re-established routines but also represented something which the young person would not reject. The services had not the capacity to offer any significant degree of off-site teaching – if this happened at all, it would be part of a package. It was only in the most extreme of circumstances, in order to stop a foster placement breaking down, that service teachers would provide the child's sole educational input; all were wary of becoming a 'third tier education provision' rather than a facilitator of integration and inclusion. However, in one authority particularly, they were being increasingly forced into this for lack of any alternatives within the LEA. A senior officer in this authority was concerned about it, feeling that they should establish firmly that they existed to help others rather than to do their job for them. There are, clearly, resource issues here. These will be discussed in chapter seven. One service manager was concerned that any alternative provision should, ideally, be within the education system and accountable to the local authority.

Individual Education Plans

In some of the case study authorities, looked-after children had Individual Education Plans. These are not the same as those related to pupils with special educational needs under the terms of the Code of Practice but are similar in terms of processes involved. For looked-after children they represented a powerful tool for planning, recording, reviewing and evaluating input from the support services; they were working towards all looked-after young people having these but, obviously, implementing this was a slow process particularly as social workers, schools and carers all had to be aware of the policy. A foster carer who was a vocal advocate for these plans told amusing anecdotes of how she badgered both special needs co-ordinators and satellite social services offices, none of whom was familiar with education plans and who took the superior line with her, suggesting that she was imagining the whole business!

Other supportive initiatives

There was a clutch of other, smaller-scale initiatives, some of which might only be undertaken by one team member or in one area. The following shows the range of support offered. Education support staff:

- assisted in the formation of homework clubs in children's homes and there was also a case where a member of staff took a boy to the team's centre to do his homework to avoid conflict in his foster home
- advised residential homes on suitable reference books, fiction and educational software. The wide benefits of working with looked-after young people through paired reading schemes has been documented (see Topping and Lindsay, 1992)
- tutored a looked-after girl who, encouragingly, had been moved up to a higher set for a particular subject but then found that she could not cope as the work was more advanced and the school had not been able to help her catch up
- attended to practical difficulties so that the girl could be 'included' and did not stand out – for example, ingredients for food technology.

One service did a lot of outdoor pursuits work, particularly with young people who were out of school; it was considered that this enhanced their confidence and social skills. A senior manager in this authority, however, wondered whether this was the most effective use of specialists' time.

In another authority, a member of the support service was accompanying a year 7 pupil on a school residential course; the school refused to allow the pupil to attend without this support but it was essential for her to be included so that she had the same experiences as her peers (she had just transferred from primary school) and she was not made to feel different. In relation to this incident, it is worth making the point that schools were often not prepared to take difficult looked-after young people away on residentials. But the experience away from 'safe' contexts is very often one that these young people need (as any young person) but which they have rarely had the opportunity for. The following story was told by some foster parents.

'The school does not believe in him. He wanted to do Duke of Edinburgh [award scheme] but the school wouldn't take him on camp. So we arranged a place for him on a holiday camp and said nothing to the people in charge. We phoned afterwards and asked for their comments and they said that though he seemed a bit odd there were no problems ... Then the third day back at school we had a phone call asking for his removal.'

The foster parents' contention was that the boy responded to expectations in the environment. They pointed out that he was verbally and physically violent at school but at home he never swore and 'behaves perfectly normally'. Their perception was that this was because 'we're middle-aged and middle-class and have grown-up children' and that he behaved accordingly. Clearly, this is a simplistic analysis and there is counterfactual evidence that young people can be unproblematic at school but difficult at home; however, it also contains some truth. Young people, carers and support service teachers all commented on the effects of certain teachers, for example, who would say something positive about them or give them the benefit of the doubt. We return once again to two point: first, one of the most important things to do is to change people's expectations and perceptions of young people in the care system; second, that young people are partners in the enterprise – there is evidence to show that in many cases they are willing partners once they are accepted into this partnership. Too often, it would seem, they are excluded from it by virtue of prejudice.

Some case examples

There was ample evidence of structured support – for example, over exclusion episodes or in relation to induction, as reported above. However, there was also telling evidence of what appeared to be insignificant, almost trivial incidents which could, nevertheless, have a disproportionate effect. It is almost as though, with extremely vulnerable young people, both negative and positive incidents have far-reaching consequences when, with a more stable, secure and advantaged child, they would pass by unnoticed. This puts a tremendous weight of responsibility on all those working with these young people and makes a strong case for their being aware both of the characteristics of being looked-after and of the specific pupils who are looked-after: one interviewee made the point, 'it is no good raising teachers' awareness if you are not going to tell them to whom the facts apply'.

In each of the following incidents, the underpinning strategy was working with the child's strengths, ensuring success 'that others would recognise' and giving praise. This, for those who have been used to failure and disapproval, can be perceived as something of a miracle or a breakthrough.

A support teacher was a regular visitor to a primary school and had established team teaching with a class teacher. He did a project on Time with the whole class, as part of which the class designed clocks. He then took out Susan, the looked-after pupil with whom he was working, to make the two best designs. One of the finished products went in the

> classroom and the other went in the head teacher's study. Not only was her morale boosted, in that she had been chosen to make the clocks, had them admired and then had them displayed as a permanent and public reminder of her achievement, but she also at last learnt to tell the time – she thought that it was odd that she had made a clock but could not use it!

In another primary school, a boy made leather keyrings for all the staff in a withdrawal session with a support service worker. The staff responded positively and said things like: 'Surely you didn't make this, it's brilliant!'. This gave him confidence and gave him much needed success. The support teacher said wryly: 'I'm sure that the next time he exploded he wasn't excluded because the head teacher had one of his keyrings!'

On both these occasions the support teacher was working with the child on a withdrawal basis. As with special education, there are times when it is appropriate to do this rather than support in the classroom. Furthermore, it gave the opportunity to talk through things with a troubled child. Some interviewees pointed out that a child might well know a support teacher far better than a social worker: not only did s/he spend more time with the teacher but the teacher was present when the young person was actually facing the difficulty – confronting a mainstream teacher, for example. They could work through the incident together, the support teacher having first-hand knowledge of the situation. This rarely happened with social workers, who would only be able to work with the child in retrospect.

Another case example illustrated how an 'educational' intervention by the support teacher saved both the classroom and, perhaps more importantly, the family situation.

> At school, Peter, a child 'in need', was very disorganised. He had learning difficulties and, if told to get a pencil he was fine, but if told to get a pencil and a ruler he could not cope. The support teacher noticed these organisational problems and worked with Peter on them, using various relevant materials. He also worked with the special needs co-ordinator and the class teacher. The former was good but had not picked up on Peter's organisational problems – she was extremely overworked and had not come across the relevant materials; the latter was keen to learn and started giving Peter lists of things to get. The strategy was successful and his organisational skills began to improve. Meanwhile, at home, Peter was suffering physical abuse. His natural father and his new partner did not realise that Peter had learning difficulties and thought that he was just being naughty: 'He is told to come in at 6.00 and doesn't come

till 8.00' (Peter could not tell the time); and 'we tell him to go to the shop for x and y and he returns with a and b'. When it was explained to them, by the support teacher who was able to forge a relationship with the couple, that Peter was not naughty but simply was not able, unaided, to follow instructions and so forth, the couple became sympathetic and understanding 'and helped the boy rather than thrashing him'.

Although it might be argued that a social worker could have explained the boy's problems to his parents, a number of interviewees observed that support service teachers, having no axe to grind, as it were, representing no statutory authority – as an education welfare officer might, for example – and being entirely 'pro' the young person, were very often in an optimal, at times unique, position to forge a relationship with parents who were experiencing difficulties in their responses to their children. It is true to say that everyone interviewed spoke of their trust of the support service teachers. Of a head of service a social services senior manager said: 'he's straightforward and honest – you can trust him'; foster and residential carers made similar comments about team members. Social workers themselves admitted that sometimes education support workers could do business with a child in a unique way as they did not have to focus on the specific care issues to which the child might be resistant.

Indeed, 'taking the flak' off others was something that a number of interviewees referred to. Carers were sometimes disillusioned by the reception that they received from schools – particularly those schools which did not respect them as fellow-professionals working on the child's case. Foster carers in particular spoke of feeling upset when they were taken to task in no uncertain terms by head teachers for their foster child's misdemeanours. It was a comfort to know that the education support teacher would, as appropriate, go to see the head teacher on their behalf. Furthermore, an experienced foster carer said that although young people would grumble about the support teachers, they were the first people that they would ask for if something went wrong 'because they know that they'll sort it out'. 'The kids have a special relationship with them – they're social workers and teachers wrapped into one.'

Praise and reward

Unsurprisingly, given that the impetus behind the services was the acknowledgement of what looked-after young people could do, the services put a lot of store on rewarding young people, both doing this themselves and encouraging residential and foster carers to do likewise. In three of the authorities the support service organised annual awards ceremonies: prestigious events where any educational achievement of looked-after children was recognised and celebrated. An account of one of these attended by a member of the research team is produced below – the others were very similar.

> The ceremony began at 10.45 am in the town hall, which was packed with young people, their families or carers and various professionals and guests who, while waiting, had been entertained by a jazz band. The Chief Education Officer gave an opening speech and then the awards were presented by the Lord Mayor. The young people (there were about 120) went up in alphabetical order with the professional who had nominated them. The latter stood beside the young person on stage and gave a short account of what the young person had done to achieve the award, congratulating them on good behaviour, attendance, effort and, in many cases, for significant educational achievement. The young people received certificates, badges and £15 vouchers, and had their photo taken with their nominee (usually service teachers or social workers).
>
> The youngest award winner was six, the oldest 21 – a boy who had a place on a business studies degree course. One girl had achieved four GCSEs, was starting A levels and was planning to go to university; twelve months previously she had been unable to attend the award ceremony as she had been serving a custodial sentence for offences which those who knew her said were uncharacteristic of her and a reaction to personal traumas; she had persisted with her studies in prison. Another girl had gained an NVQ in hairdressing a year before her peers; while another appeared on stage pregnant and carrying a toddler – she too had persisted with her studies and was attending a social care course.
>
> After the ceremony, the young people and their guests were entertained to a buffet lunch with further musical entertainment.

It might be asked why this was necessary: schools, after all, have prizegivings and ways of recognising achievement. Again, it needs to be remembered that young people who are looked-after are not 'normal', by virtue of their abnormal life experiences. While some schools are excellent in recognising what is an achievement for an individual pupil, as measured against his or her former achievement, others simply do not realise that 80 per cent attendance for a looked-after pupil who had a history of non-attendance is a remarkable achievement – something for which the young person has had to work. Similarly, a number of schools recognise alternative accreditation in key stage four (see, for example, Fletcher-Campbell, 1996). Others, however, celebrate standard GCSE passes and forget to acknowledge the achievement represented by a basic skills certificate. Thus some forum that assures that looked-after young people's achievements are publicly recognised is essential. Furthermore, it is important to gather the achieving looked-after young people together both to give them personal encouragement, to provide peer role models, and to make a public declaration that *looked-after children do achieve*. No one at a school prize-giving is going to know that the pupil is looked-after; in this context it is neither desirable nor appropriate that looked-after pupils are marked out. However, for local politicians, the public at large, potential employers and, in many cases, professionals, it is important to advertise the achievement. A number of residential unit managers, for example, spoke of the local prejudice against opening children's homes – the immediate thought of neighbours was that there was going to be trouble and that the residents would be delinquent. There is still much misinformation to be dispelled.

Support service staff also put high value on using praise to motivate schools. They would tell them that 'you're doing a grand job' where the school was holding on to a pupil displaying difficult behaviour, for example. One support teacher said: 'I get under the skin of staff and appeal to their better natures!' If any teacher had shown positive behaviour towards a looked-after child, they would tell them how much this was valued; or they would tell Mr Smith how pleased they were that he was a looked-after child's form tutor, head of year or whatever, so that he would be given the message that they trusted him to deal sensitively with the child. Looked-after children may, or may not, be more sensitive than their peers but their perception was – and perceptions are important in that they inform responses – that they were 'picked on'. Thus a slightly more favourable approach from a teacher could readjust this perception; whether or not it was correctly formed in the first place is irrelevant.

As regards using praise and developing the sort of culture which looked at what young people can do – the 'fundamental task' referred to in chapter three – the following anecdote is incisive. A foster father was telling of an incident with his foster daughter, who was in her last year at primary school; she had suffered sustained and severe abuse, responding by exhibiting violent behaviour.

> 'I said to her: "If you have four really good days at school and one bad one, what do people remember?" She replied, "the bad one".'

What would happen if people first remembered the good ones?

Training

Formal training

All services were involved in training of some sort. In some cases this involved formal sessions with area staff either from one discipline (for example, headteachers) or from a number of agencies – as with any in-service training, there are advantages and disadvantages of these two approaches. An example of a regional training course is given below.

Invited *participants* included: service, family centre and children's homes managers; head teachers and governors of secondary and special schools; colleges of further education; officers from the area education office, education welfare service and LEA education support service; parents and carers; and voluntary organisations.

The *programme* included a session of the developing role of the social services department (in the light of the Children Act), on schools' perceptions of problems with looked-after children, and on background information about education and looked-after children. Workshop sessions identified key issues at grassroots level and discussed what delegates were going to do about them. A final session considered a joint action plan.

One *outcome* of the training day was that a steering group was established, comprising a primary and a secondary headteacher, a representative from further education, a service manager, a residential manager, an educational psychologist, an education welfare officer and the head of the social services education support service.

A second *outcome* was that an inter-agency partnership service level agreement was established. This comprised:

- underpinning principles (e.g. curriculum entitlement and equal opportunities)
- purposes (e.g. to increase accountability, view the needs of children as joint concerns, enhance open communication, clarify roles and responsibilities)
- an action plan to effect these principles and purposes (e.g. the production of information manual, guidance for school on social services' referral procedures, all schools to have a named person to take lead responsibility for looked-after pupils)
- induction and training opportunities
- local policy (e.g. all schools with pupils in residential care to have a copy of that home's education policy and to have a support plan for each looked-after pupil; schools to provide the SSD office with a copy of their current prospectus)
- arrangements for quality assurance and review.

Another authority was piloting a training module in conjunction with a local college.

> The course was directed at social workers and carers (both foster and residential). Attendance was one half day per week over a twelve week period. The programme included:
> - understanding the educational context of young people looked-after
> - special educational needs, admissions, attendance, exclusions and alternative provision
> - promoting the educational opportunities of young people looked-after.

A third authority was developing INSET for schools; 'ready-made packages are always extremely attractive to busy teachers!' and developing a modular course for social workers, delivered by service managers and leading to a National Vocational Qualification (NVQ).

All carers spoke of the difficulties of attending formal training sessions. With foster carers, the difficulty was actually getting out in the evening – one explained how, having particularly difficult children, she always had to be on call and was always having to interrupt the session by going home to deal with a crisis. With residential carers, the problem was both overall staffing and shift rotas. In recognition of this, one education support service was offering a development programme for carers at the residential home – possibly using staff meeting time. The basic course involved three one-hour sessions which aimed to increase staff awareness of education issues and how best to address them.

> Session one: the basic legal position, the duties of LEAs, schools and parents; the implications of circular 13/94 and the SSI/Ofsted report
>
> Session two: the Code of Practice, exclusions, and education otherwise
>
> Session three: work experience, careers guidance and general issues.

Informal training

Thus, in many ways, the most influential training was that delivered as a task and undertaken in collaboration with colleagues. One service manager said that, in any case, formal training was poorly received in his area – 'it looks too dictatorial' – and that working with people was far more effective. An immense amount of staff development (and also personal development for foster carers) went on as service teachers just went about their business, particularly as that business in the main involved working with others and facilitating others to create environments which would integrate and include young people looked-after. Service staff really need all the skills of mentoring and guidance.

After care? Post-16 careers

If young people are to be encouraged to achieve and succeed at school – rather than merely to tolerate being contained there – the logical consequence is that they should proceed to further or higher education. Traditionally, research shows that young people in the care system have rarely progressed to further education or training and are, consequently, disproportionately represented in those who are unemployed (see, for example, Biehal *et al.*, 1992; Broad, 1994; Aftercare Consortium, 1996). All the support services, although having a brief for young people of statutory school age (sometimes further restricted to those of secondary school age) were anxious that those exceptions became less exceptional, as it were, and opportunities for further and higher education were taken seriously by young people looked-after. The fact that careers evenings were held to inform young people of opportunities has already been mentioned above. Service managers were anxious that there should be structures by which young people would have contact with further education – rather than it depending on a particularly committed carer, for example. Young people were often introduced to college via the packages of education designed for them at key stage four – in many cases it was hoped that 'street-wise' young people would respond to the more adult world of college. One support service team was trying to ensure that all young people in key stage four who were excluded and with whom the service was working, would do at least one GCSE and have a Record of Achievement 'with something worthwhile in it'. Again, the latter is an entitlement – there is no special practice here – but, once again, it was an entitlement which looked-after young people often missed out on. As schools needed educating about the experience of being looked-after so did colleges. Colleges had as many false assumptions about students who had been in the care system as some schools did. One practitioner spoke of the way in which one college always used to put able looked-after students on vehicle maintenance courses for students with learning difficulties.

One service manager had recently negotiated, with a local institute of higher education, a compact for the raising of participation rates within higher education: the message was, 'Looked after children go to university'. A copy of the document went to all service managers and residential children's

Post 16 edt

homes. As national statistics relating to participation rates alter – now, for example, nearly a third of the 18+ cohort go to higher education – so must expectations of looked-after young people. The normal situation should surely be that we challenge why they do not go rather than be amazed when they do. The model of the compact was similar, structurally, to that for other support: essentially, it involved partnership, with clear roles and responsibilities. It was noteworthy in that it was recognised that a continuation of additional support might be necessary for this group of young people. As elsewhere, positive discrimination is sometimes necessary in order to ensure equality of opportunity: the morality of simply awarding a place to a young person looked-after without considering whether s/he might need complementary support in order to 'take the ball and run' is questionable. It is worth briefly outlining the compact as it illustrates this complementary support: as with schools, the institute of higher education was not left alone – when it might have anticipated problems. Also, it demonstrates that real demands were being made of the young people concerned.

As well as specifying course entry criteria (as for any student), the *institute of higher education* would:

- work with the education support service in presenting a positive view of further and higher education to students (recognising that many of these young people would not immediately consider further and higher education, as a young person from another background might automatically)
- work with the education support service in refining criteria for the assessment of the student's performance (recognising that conventional accreditation may not have been possible)
- support the student in finding accommodation (many young people receive support from family and friends in this)
- support the student after entry with a programme of tutor interviews and with help tailored to his/her requirements (recognising that some students may have been accustomed to this support from the education support service, may have few general support networks through family and friends, and may need help in establishing study patterns and acquiring study skills).

The *support service* would, *inter alia*:

- identify a group of students (in the future, participation could be established as a long-term goal for pupils at school)
- draw up an individual action plan (continuing the practice established at school level)
- support the students in relation to attendance and punctuality and in meeting course deadlines (a matter of attending to routines and continuing work done previously)
- support under-achieving students with counselling and individual attention (ensuring that other things did not get in the way – again, as at school)
- ensure that the student has a record of achievement.

As well as fulfilling basic entry criteria (which might, or might not, be conventional qualifications) and reaching satisfactory coursework assessment (i.e., there were no academic compromises), the student would:

- be regular and punctual in attending college for the whole of the course (personal responsibility)
- hold a record of achievement or similar assessment profile which demonstrates development through the agreed individual action plan, and a good response to the agreed non-examination curriculum (the student was thus encouraged to conceive progressing to a degree through a series of planned steps and action points – rather than be daunted by the prospect of three years' work).

The service manager was planning to engage in similar negotiations with further education providers.

Some authorities had been successful in approaching businesses for support. Sometimes this was in the form of kind – for example, sponsorship of rewards for achievement; sometimes in the form of sponsorship of special projects; at others, in the form of offers of work experience placements. Again, this was on the margins of the NFER research brief but is relevant insofar as it is another logical consequence of taking education seriously – the concept of *progression* is critical to all young people but, in the past, has been neglected as far as looked-after young people are concerned.   For further information on career and work opportunities for young people looked-after, see Action on Aftercare Consortium (1996).

Summary

♦ Services perceived themselves as mediators between education and social services departments;

♦ services considered that it was essential to work through other agents;

♦ services considered that they were in a unique position to mediate on account of their overview of cases, objectivity, technical knowledge, experience in the field, and their understanding of procedures and structures in both education and social service departments;

♦ services also perceived themselves as informers, gathering and disseminating data for managers, officers, carers, teachers and education providers;

♦ their function included attending meetings and reviews as appropriate, in order to keep educational issues high on the agenda;

♦ education support service managers were concerned to collect useful data at local authority level but encountered difficulties with incompatible management information systems, data collection methods and categorisations;

♦ service managers were often a source of information regarding resources available in the area;

♦ the case work of team members could be on an intensive or 'holding' basis and included visiting and working with young people, carers, schools and professional colleagues;

♦ one service had instituted a scheme whereby each new referral underwent an intensive scrutiny of his or her needs in the classroom in order to analyse exactly where support should be targeted or present practice readjusted;

♦ few services wished to offer direct teaching though they were offering it in some cases in default of other provision;

♦ in some cases, services were involved in developing teaching or pastoral skills of ordinary teachers working with young people;

- services were often engaged in arranging educational packages for young people at key stage 4;

- education plans, to establish educational aims and objectives for a looked-after young person, were used in some authorities; these were additional, but related, to any plans written under the terms of the Code of Practice;

- members of support teams engaged in many other initiatives such as homework clubs, advising on library materials and software, outdoor pursuits, and supporting young people who might have been excluded from residential courses;

- there was considerable evidence that apparently trivial incidents could have disproportionate effects on vulnerable young people, both advantageously and disadvantageously;

- several authorities had formal award ceremonies to acknowledge the achievement of young people who were looked-after;

- all services engaged in some degree of formal training of professional colleagues across agencies; in a few areas, accredited courses were being developed;

- all services were involved with much informal training 'on-the-job';

- service providers were beginning to look at young people's chances post-16, and were considering progression to further education and training; collaboration was sought with higher education and business.

CHAPTER 5
THE CARERS

Introduction

This chapter will examine the part played by carers in the education of the young people for whom they were responsible. It will describe their perceptions of education and what they did to support the educational placements of the children, and will identify the way in which specialist services helped them to fulfil their responsibilities. Issues common to both residential carers and foster carers will be considered as well as the particular problems associated with residential care.

The carers involved in the research

In chapter one it was pointed out that the residential and foster carers interviewed in the course of the NFER research may not necessarily be representative of all carers in all local authorities. They were suggested by senior managers in the social services as being examples of people who took education seriously, regarded it as part of their responsibilities and were experienced in addressing problems with young people's schooling. In most cases, they had been involved with the discrete educational services available for looked-after young people. The researchers were aware that they had the privilege of meeting some of the most articulate, committed, experienced and able carers in the case study authorities.

The carers themselves were very varied in terms of background and experience.

Foster carers

Foster homes visited ranged from those on run-down council estates to those in leafy, professional neighbourhoods; the range of occupations, where these applied, was broad (from manual work, through middle management, to senior management in a large international company) as was that of their experience of fostering. Some were university-educated while others said that they had acquired literacy skills after they had left school but were determined that their foster children should have an easier path. Some of the foster parents had seen all their own children through university, others had children still at primary or secondary school, while others had very young children of their own; they thus had different degrees of experience with the educational system. There was also a range of experience as regards contact with different types of school: for example, some had experience of independent schools, both for their own and for foster children; others had preferences for denominational schools, either for their own or their foster children.

As regards the recruitment of foster carers more generally, all the authorities visited were experiencing difficulties. Some managers attributed this to competition with other neighbouring authorities; others to levels of resourcing. The latter affected the situation in two ways. First, in terms of the small weekly amount received by 'ordinary' foster carers (i.e. those other than in special adolescent projects, where payments were higher and it was regarded as a job): social services officers remarked that people simply would not put up with aggressive, difficult youngsters in their homes for such minimal reward. Second, in terms of the support available for foster carers: more correctly, the concern was that support was lacking and that foster placements might be maintained if carers were able to draw on more support, advice and respite care.

There were so many variables in terms of matching ages, locations, ethnicity and so forth, that trying to add in that of educational background or suitability was simply not possible. Previous research found this to be the case and there is now evidence that it remains. One fostering team manager said that, although the importance of maintaining a school placement was regarded as critical within the team, considering 'educational suitability' when allocating foster placements had to be a low priority. Her further comments were as follows:

> 'However, we wouldn't put a low achieving child with a foster carer who put a high priority on educational success. In training, we would identify how supportive of education the foster parent was going to be. Equally, we wouldn't put a high achieving child with a family who wouldn't give a quiet place for homework.'

In many ways, it was discouraging that the 'training' provided by this team did not include discussion of the responsibilities of foster carers – for example, that provision for homework would be an expectation, and that foster carers should provide for and work with the child's educational needs whether these be associated with high or low achievement. There is, clearly, much awareness raising still to be done. The encouraging thing was that the interviewee said that if they picked up that a foster carer would be unable to deal with issues to do with the child's school, her team would alert the social worker so that s/he could assume more responsibility in this area.

Residential carers

The overall profile of residential carers was similarly varied. In residential units, much depended on the unit manager, who was influential in establishing the ethos of the home – as will be discussed below. The unit managers, all of whom had been recommended as 'wanting to tackle educational issues' came from a range of backgrounds. Interestingly, none attributed their emphasis on the importance of education to their own social work training (although the internal 'training' or staff development of the specialist services had often been a critical factor). One, for example, said:

'I suppose it was because of my background. I had been in residential for ten years and then went to work in a Child Guidance clinic, doing joint work with Health. I worked in a clinic where the educational psychologists also worked, so education was part of my environment and it was a matter of seeing the results where they were working – not part of my social work training.'

In other cases, it was a slower, more developmental process as their way of managing the care side became, as it were, more 'educational' – see below.

Within residential staff teams, younger staff became involved with education by virtue of the expectations made of them by their manager, by following the routines of the unit, for example; or by being given formal responsibility for educational matters. Sometimes it was just by critical, concerned observation. A young graduate, but professionally unqualified, care worker employed on a temporary basis, said:

'I was concerned that they weren't getting enough support with their homework and a lot of them have had SATs in the last couple of weeks, and all I was aware of was that when I had exams and I was living at home, I used to revise and go downstairs and my mum would test me. Now they haven't had that and I think they should. If they don't want it, that's up to them but they should have had the opportunity to be asked, and although there is not time to give that one-to-one attention for a prolonged period, just half an hour could have made a big difference. So last week we decided to try to set up a homework club ... they are not expected to do it [homework] all by themselves. Because I wasn't expected to and I don't see why they should have to ... I had my parents there every night saying 'have you done your homework?' And so I know to me it is very important and I know I wouldn't have reached where I am now if I hadn't had that support.'

This member of staff worked in a residential unit where education was 'on the agenda' and so her ideas were taken up and supported. This institutional support was apparent in all the residential homes visited: the importance of education was embedded into routines, albeit to varying degrees, and did not depend on whether a particular key worker thought education to be important for a particular young person.

Again, what was the overall position with regard to the recruitment of residential carers? The situation remains similar, in practice, to that when the previous NFER research into the education of children in care was undertaken. Many residential staff are unqualified and seek the work after experience of a range of other employment. The case study authorities, and, indeed, individual unit managers, differed in their departmental policies as regards staff qualifications. Some were promoting internal training schemes; one case study authority, with a reputation for its seriousness and positive initiatives as regards staff development for all levels of staff, was including sessional workers in formal training at authority level. Elsewhere, managers saw opportunities for NVQs delivered by service managers.

Unit managers valued staff training for three main reasons, on which they put different degrees of emphasis. First, it enhanced the work of the unit; second, the fact that staff were engaging in continuing education and training gave a message to the young people that adults did do this and thought it important; third, staff with qualifications gave a positive role model to the young people in their care. Others saw the issue of staff training differently. Three examples follow.

> *Manager A* realised that one of her weaknesses was staff development and, having worked hard on securing the young people's educational placements, was turning her attention to staff. She rejected the idea of formal induction, making the point that staff had such different backgrounds that they learnt in different ways and at different paces. She wanted to be able to present them with challenges and opportunities as and when they were ready.
>
> *Manager B* put high value on having qualified staff as role models for residents. He considered that it was important that staff should have high expectations of the young people and felt that that was why it was important for staff to be qualified: 'it doesn't matter what in, it could be a degree in theology, but they should be able to function at a higher level. It's difficult to get someone who's only worked in a supermarket or been a rigger, or dropped out as a sapper, to take education seriously.' Although this sentiment is debatable, and some of the evidence would prove counterfactual, the basic point that the manager is making is important: young people who are looked-after need introducing to alternatives. This is discussed further below.

Manager C favoured in-service training, both on-the-job and in terms of staff being facilitated to pursue qualifications by part-time study. Having the opportunity to make a new appointment, she was seeking a qualified member of staff so that this person could take on some management responsibility, freeing her to engage in more developmental work. Interestingly, this unit had a development plan which included education.

Common characteristics of carers

All the foster and residential carers interviewed had more in common than they had in variance: all were wholeheartedly positive about the importance of education and were determined to 'fight' to ensure that the young people for whom they were responsible got the best deal possible, as it were. All admitted their own strengths and weaknesses in educational matters, were willing to seek and accept advice, and were keen to work in collaboration with support workers and schools in order to secure educational placements. All were confident as regards their role in education. In some cases, they had acquired skills in negotiating with schools regarding places for their young people; in others, they were aware of how their work could complement that of the education support workers who might be the more appropriate people to do the actual negotiation. In all cases, however, they felt empowered, usually on account of the professional support from the specialist services on which they could draw and rely. They showed that foster carers can make a positive difference. The comment was often made that 'foster carers feel that they haven't the skills' – there was research evidence that this need not be the case.

The young people for whom they cared

In all cases, the carers interviewed were responsible for some of the most damaged young people whose care presented enormous difficulties. Many were in assessment placements or in foster homes where, as one carer put it, 'we'll take anything'. Although the research team had not specifically asked for such cases, it welcomed the fact that the profile of young people was as it was as it is not possible for other carers to feel that their colleagues involved in this piece of research had any 'easy options'. Some case studies of young people are presented throughout this report, but, overall, the following comments set the scene:

> '[This authority's looked-after] kids don't just nick Mars bars, you know; they rape and stab people ...' *(social services senior manager)*
>
> 'As a foster parent you think "no one's going to have a kid like this ... no one knows what I'm going through"' *(foster parent)*
>
> 'And he's a boy who kicks doors in and attacks other kids just for the hell of it ...' *(residential care worker)*

(In both the later, specific cases, educational intervention with the young people concerned had been 'successful'.) The cases discussed with the researchers included young people involved in prostitution, the drug scene, joy-riding and care theft, murder, sexual abuse, and violence in home, school and/or the community. They were, thus, not merely what one social worker said were sometimes termed 'sad' children; they could, he said, on an uninformed analysis, be termed 'bad' – though the truth is that they were, undoubtedly, 'damaged'. The point at issue is that they were not children whose natural parents were merely unable for whatever reason to care for them and who settled happily and securely in long-term foster placements. The young people in residential care were generally regarded as 'unfosterable' at the time and many of the adolescents involved in the research were in special fostering projects and schemes – they were, again, the most difficult young people. No excuses can, thus, be made on the grounds that they presented no challenge as regards education or care placements. The majority of the carers interviewed were dealing with permanent or temporary exclusion, or reintegration after a lengthy period when the young person had not attended school. None of the carers had any illusions about the challenges, the stresses and strains, and the apparently insurmountable difficulties; but all showed that with co-operation, determination and the right support at the right time, progress could be made, and positive educational experiences could be effected which, in turn, helped to stabilise the care situation and the young people's personal lives. In all cases, educational placements were perceived as having a profound effect on care placements – and *vice versa*.

Clearly, the cases presented are not claimed to be representative of the looked-after population as a whole. Focusing on some of the most extreme cases, as this report does, distorts the picture and neglects the fact that there are many children who are looked-after who, though they may have complex emotional difficulties (and we all have emotional difficulties to some extent) do not present behavioural difficulties, are 'unnoticeable' at school in that they fit in and learn apparently 'normally' and do not seem to 'need' any specific intervention. This particular piece of research did not explicitly explore the educational experiences of these young people although important issues are raised elsewhere (see chapters two and seven) about the way in which intervention might facilitate greater levels of achievement and attainment.

The majority of the carers were looking after adolescents, although there were some children of primary school age involved; one of the residential homes offered specialist provision for children aged up to the age of 10 on admission and there were children under the age of 11 in another of the residential units visited. Most of the social services departments in the case study authorities had a policy of not placing younger children in residential care (this policy did, in fact, sometimes clash with policy of colleagues in the education department as regards placement in residential special schools – as is discussed elsewhere in this report).

The practical impact of education on care placements

As mentioned above, the educational careers of many of the young people discussed in the course of the NFER research were characterised by suspension and exclusion from school; this particular issue is dealt with in more detail elsewhere (see chapter six). Its relevance here is the effect that it had on carers.

Foster homes

Social services officers responsible for home-finding or fostering referred to the fact that many potential foster carers would only accept young people who had a full-time school place. Essentially, foster carers believed that this was the child's entitlement, *qua* pupil, and it was a positive and beneficial experience for the young person. They pointed out that many looked-after children, on account of their previous domestic experiences, lack social skills; they need to mix with a broad range of their peers and have the opportunity to form friendships with children from a variety of home circumstances. More practically, there were logistical problems. Some foster carers (though not usually those on the specialist adolescent schemes) had full-time jobs; others needed the time and space during the day to do the housework and the shopping; others needed time with their own young children, particularly if they were not yet at school. Part-time schooling, though regarded as 'better than nothing' interfered with these routines (which is why a full-time, or full-time equivalent, placement was often a requirement). A foster mother said that if a child was only out of the house for a couple of hours at a time, this disrupted her day and reduced the time available to go shopping, or whatever. There were further difficulties when foster carer's 'free' time was taken up when transport did not turn up or was delayed.

More importantly, perhaps, was the very obvious fact that many of the young people were extremely demanding in terms of their behaviour; because of their past experiences, they tended to be attention-seeking and to need a considerable degree of supervision, for their own and others' safety. Quite simply, foster carers needed a break in order to restore their energies for when the child returned from school. One foster mother said: 'When you have a child for seven days a week, 24 hours a day, you just get worn out and it all feels like an uphill struggle'. Another couple, who had committed themselves to the long-term fostering of a very demanding primary-school aged girl who exhibited violence, having been the subject of considerable physical and emotional neglect, spoke of the stress of continually being rung up by the school to remove the girl. They admitted that, at times, 'we went out for days at a time so that we would not be called upon'. (The issue of schools 'using' carers in this way – to remove difficult pupils – will be discussed elsewhere.)

Social services managers were acutely aware that if school placements broke down, then care placements did also. This had resource and administrative implications over and above the critical effect of yet another 'failure' and further disruption for the child concerned. Thus it was in the interests of social services to support families where children were at home during the day. In one case, for example, a respite carer had been put in to a foster home to care for a young boy presenting extreme behaviour during the day in order to relieve the foster mother.

In another case, a boy was both on the verge of care and at the point of exclusion from his primary school on account of unacceptable behaviour. He had no statement and the school would only keep him on condition that he went home at lunchtimes: the lunchtime supervisors could not cope with him and both he and other pupils were in danger. However, the family situation was such that the boy's mother could not cope with him at lunchtime so, in order to prevent the school placement breaking down, the social worker put in a family aid worker to cover lunchtimes at the school: 'it was in our interests to do so'. When questioned, the social worker said that the strategy of using family aids to assist pupils in school had been used by her colleagues before.

These are but two examples of many which make the point that some social workers are serious about young people's schooling and do not dismiss it as irrelevant, as they are sometimes accused of doing. Other interventions will be discussed elsewhere.

Residential children's homes

Residential carers interviewed also saw the positive benefits of young people attending school. In addition to those articulated by foster carers (issues of entitlement, for example) residential workers also pointed out that school broke the institutionalisation of a children's home and gave opportunities for new friends and structures; young people on a care order, for example, might not have home leave and thus be isolated from ordinary family life.

The impact of young people having no school place was similar in residential children's homes: there were resource and administrative implications and the ethos of the home was affected. The way in which residential units were transformed, from places where no resident went to school to places where there was 100 per cent attendance, will be discussed below. Meanwhile, the focus is in on what motivates staff to secure educational placements.

Social services staff spoke of the fact that many problems arose in residential units not necessarily because the residents were particularly disruptive but because they were bored – 'and then they'll set fire to things as a form of excitement'. One unit manager determined to do something about education when, a new appointee, she came in and saw 'the staff sitting round the kitchen table with the kids from nine to three trying to educate them'. A residential carer spoke of the way staff 'racked their brains to know how to occupy them', while another said:

> 'We don't do the kids a good service. If [the social services' education support service] is not involved, we make up spelling tests and sums. We say during the day no TV and 'sit and do these sums we've just thought of'. It's awful for them ... after a week with nothing to do they go off into town and hang about.'

Residential carers, as foster carers, had other things to do during the day. This might be administration, for example, or it might be outreach work. Several managers spoke of the deleterious effect on preventative work in the community which was caused by having to keep the staff in the unit all day to supervise residents out of school. The issue of effectiveness was implicit here although it was not explicitly articulated by interviewees: as seen from the comments above, staff were very aware of the fact that they were totally failing young people during the school day, were merely containing them and were not allowing them to pursue worthwhile educational projects. The way in which staff were spending their time was not as purposeful as it might be were they engaged on a specific outreach activity, for example. Issues such as this will be considered in greater depth in the final chapter of this report.

As with foster homes, additional support was given to residential homes to relieve pressure where residents were at home all day. In some cases this was put in by a senior service manager; at others, the unit manager would use the budget to provide one-to-one work with a resident, particularly where that resident was in danger. One unit manager spoke of the tensions arising with a particularly difficult adolescent boy excluded from school; the situation was exacerbated by the fact that there were few residential staff able to cope with him. The unit manager himself, outside his managerial brief, took on some of the responsibility for the boy, playing football with him, for example, or taking him off-site in order to relieve the tensions he was causing. But he worried about the messages that this was conveying to other residents: the way to get additional attention (craved by many young people who are looked-after) or more interesting activities was, clearly, to display extreme behaviour.

Residential staff were all in agreement that when residents felt secure and were achieving at school, the atmosphere in the home in the evenings and at weekends was much happier. This was for very obvious reasons: they had something to talk about when they came home, they met a fresh group of adults and peers, they were doing what other young people did and they were purposefully occupied. One unit manager, who had transformed the unit from a place where there was nil attendance to one where there was often 100 per cent attendance, spoke of the high point of the day when the residents came home and sat around the kitchen table, 'all in their different school uniforms', and chatted about what had happened during the day at school. How such a state of affairs is achieved and maintained by carers will now be explored.

Foster carers' intervention in the education of the children they looked after

The effect of the specialist support services

The various foster carers interviewed had different ideas about the extent to which their responsibilities extended and what they felt confident to do. However, what was common was the fact that they were clear about what needed to be done and the means by which it had been achieved. All, without exception, spoke of the extreme value of the specialist support services and held them in very high regard. All carers were asked by the researchers to identify difficulties with the service. None, in any of the case study authorities, could think of anything, although senior managers were sometimes able to identify ways in which the service could expand, and its limitations caused by financial stringency. Encomia were genuine, readily forthcoming and unrehearsed.

Foster carers particularly stressed the reliability of the teams; the fact that they did what they said they would do; were available without appointment, often running an advice line at the end of the phone; were flexible in the way they worked; and were utterly trustworthy and straightforward in their dealings. They welcomed the teams' particular expertise in integration and knowledge of the statutory position regarding exclusion. One foster mother remarked: 'We know where we are with the education support service whereas we never see the social workers'. Elsewhere, 'they're brilliant' and 'they're worth their weight in gold' were typical comments; one foster carer said: 'I've worked with all members of the team now and I haven't a bad word to say of any of them'. All were able to give examples of where interventions from the service had secured integration or inclusion and were able to articulate 'success' in terms of individual cases.

More particularly, some were grateful for the support of team workers when negotiating with schools. Although the schools actually visited as part of the research (see chapter six) were all recommended for such things as having a positive attitude to pupils who were looked-after, for co-operating in their integration, offering negotiated time-tables and trying at all costs to maintain their inclusion, carers had experience of a far wider range of schools and spoke about these in interview. Thus data about both helpful and unhelpful schools were collected. Foster carers mentioned that, while some schools regarded them as fellow professionals and gave them respect, others did not and treated them with little regard. In such circumstances, being able to rely on the support service teacher to engage in negotiations was a great support to the foster carers. Furthermore, although some carers looked after just one or two children, others could have as many as six (usually when they had taken sibling groups unexpectedly); when these were all at different schools, foster parents were extremely busy and often simply did not have the time to enter into lengthy negotiations – in such cases, the role of the social worker or the specialist teacher was more critical.

Where foster parents had acquired skills in negotiating with schools, most attributed this to the education support service and not to any basic foster care training. One foster mother who had, in fact, completed the pilot of a specialist module on the education of children looked-after offered by a social services education support team in conjunction with a college of higher education, commented:

> 'When people start fostering there is no part of the package which says "are you a suitable foster parent" that covers education – nothing. You're taught about all the other issues but you don't cover education. You come into it and I didn't even know about statementing kids ... if your own kid hasn't had problems or been to that sort of school where there are kids with problems you haven't a clue ... I looked through the foster parent fact file and, again, very little on the educational side.'

These comments were repeated in other authorities.

What foster parents did as regards educational support

Most of the foster parents interviewed took responsibility for finding a school place for the children they were caring for. They would often discuss this with the education support service teacher, who would probably have a wider knowledge and experience of possible schools. Whilst some would cast their net widely, others would prefer to build on existing relations with a school which they had used before, either for their own children or for previous foster children. The advantages of the latter were that channels of communication were open. Both foster and residential carers and teachers in the support services (see chapter three) spoke of the importance of establishing relationships with schools, but also of the time that this could take. One foster parent commented that she liked to keep with the same school 'so that you don't constantly have to go round explaining who you are'. It is, perhaps, all too easy to forget things like this – things which, although apparently trivial, can nevertheless be time-consuming and stressful (particularly where the reception is suspicious and hostile – see chapter six) and which do not have to be done in normal circumstances.

Particularly valued by foster carers (and also residential carers) was the way that the education support service could show foster carers alternatives:

> 'They come in and say what options there are – after getting to know the kid. They're like estate agents – looking at the market for you and they're looking inside the market because I'm on the outside of it. They're in education, on the inside, so they know much more who to talk to and the jargon to use. Ten of our kids would have been better off had they had this input – they ended up on the streets taking drugs – no job, no money and so into crime – they would at least have had the chance of doing other things.'

All foster carer were committed to being persistent advocates for their children. One couple, who had fostered over 100 children over 30 years, spoke of always pressing for something better – 'we had to have a utopia to fight for'. Others spoke of how the school would know they meant business when they rang up. One foster mother commented that she could press when the education support teacher could not. There were sometimes sensitivities – discussed in chapter 3 – in that education support teachers had to maintain relations with schools and were ever conscious of the fact that schools could, hypothetically, close their doors to them; thus they were aware of fragile boundaries. Foster parents did not have these concerns and were able to focus their energies on the particular child with whom they were currently concerned – they did not have to think about their future in the school, as it were. This is not to suggest that they necessarily did things without the support of the education service teacher: merely that it was often partnerships which actually secured action. A number of interviewees acknowledged that it was often a matter of 'playing a game'; despite the fact that they might not enjoy doing this and, in the cold light of reason, saw no reason why, when the local authority was the corporate parent, they should engage in such games, nevertheless, such strategies were sometimes effective as far as the individual child was concerned. It might be a matter of pointing out to schools that they had not fulfilled statutory obligations with regard to exclusions, for example; or reminding LEAs of their responsibilities as regards school places; or making schools aware that the child's advocates knew that the school had spare places even if it said that it was full.

All the foster parents interviewed stressed that, wherever possible, they were willing and keen to work with schools: in no case did they expect schools to work miracles on their own, nor merely to hand over the child at the school gates as it were and do nothing until s/he arrived home. Most of those interviewed were, in fact, available during the school day (as they were caring for the most troubled children who would be likely to need intensive support). Thus they would reassure schools that they would assist them when problems arose during the day. Clearly, whether foster carers' offers are taken up and used effectively to the benefit of the pupil (rather than abused) depends largely on the school's attitude and on the management of information and of the case generally – see chapter six.

Foster parents fully accepted their responsibilities as regards going to parents' evenings and reviews; ensuring that the young person had the right uniform, kit and equipment; and supervising any homework given.

Interestingly, a residential carer commented on the work that foster parents had been able to do with a boy who had just been admitted to residential care:

> 'When his ex-foster carers came to the open night, we were talking about his reading, and they said that every single night, with every foster child that they have, they spend a certain amount of time with them, and they either read to them or they have them read. Every single night without fail. When he got to them his reading was, you know, his reading has come on leaps and bounds with that one-to-one attention every single night.'

This leads to a consideration of what residential carers were able to do.

Residential carers' intervention in the education of young people they cared for

All the activities engaged in by foster parents were applicable to residential carers who also used the support services in similar ways. The distinctive data as regards residential care really rested on the way in which such activities were embedded in the routines and structures of the unit *qua* institution. This section will explore this in general terms before presenting some case studies of 'transformed' units.

Leadership from the top

All the residential units visited as part of the NFER research showed clear leadership from the top in educational matters; this was unsurprising given that recommendations of 'good practice' had been asked for. However, the style of leadership and management were not irrelevant to the way in which education was institutionalised. One service manager commented: 'once education is in the culture and the bloodstream of residential carers and homes, then it is just a question of maintenance'. Although there was evidence that 'maintenance' can be as challenging as changing the culture, the latter is certainly the foremost challenge.

In one authority, all the residential children's homes had an education policy: other authorities were considering developing these. These policies either had been, or were being, designed in collaboration with education support service staff. A senior officer in an authority where the situation *vis-à-vis* education was very variable across the different residential homes was anxious to implement a common policy across homes so that young people's chances did not depend on where they happened to be placed. An example of the policy in one residential children's home is produced below. Clear aims, reflecting the home's way of working with residents generally (this was essentially educative), were accompanied by practical examples of what staff were required to do in order that these be realised; the policy was reviewed annually within the home's business planning cycle.

Aim 1: to encourage positive attitudes towards all aspects of education
- maintaining high educational expectations
- acknowledging educational achievements
- recognising educational progress
- encouraging a wider perspective of school life
- engaging young people in informal discussions around educational matters
- discussing each young person's progress and potential at staff meetings
- maintaining a high profile of further education

Aim 2: to work in partnership with young people
- seeking and respecting their views and perceptions of education
- involving them in planning and decision-making
- improving self-esteem
- rewarding positive educational and personal achievements
- challenging unhelpful attitudes and behaviour
- helping and encouraging them to enjoy the social aspect of education
- highlighting their awareness of their own potential and future careers
- ensuring that a quiet study area and appropriate resources are available

Aim 3: to work in partnership with parents/carers
- involving them in formal decision-making and planning processes
- establishing regular dialogue concerning day-to-day educational progress
- helping them to support the child in school and further education
- supporting them in obtaining an appropriate educational placement for their child
- informing them of the educational expectations of the residential home

Aim 4: to work in partnership with local schools, colleges and universities

- Staff will liaise and meet with representatives of educational establishments as defined in the unit's 'Working in Partnership' leaflet

Aim 5: to work in partnership with the LEA

- participating in inter-agency meetings, conference and training
- being aware of the responsibilities of key education personnel
- working with the LEA in the formation of complex educational plans for individual young people

Aim 6: to work in partnership with the social services education support service

- maintaining regular contact and support as identified in the service level agreement.

In several homes, responsibility for education was delegated to a senior member of staff; in this way, not only was there someone in addition to the unit manager scrutinising education matters but 'it ensured that things got done' – there was a greater degree of accountability. Further accountability was assured by the social work practice of supervision. In all cases where there was a member of staff with delegated responsibility, the support service had 'trained' that member of staff – it is unlikely that the care officer would have been able to fulfil their responsibilities without their own staff development being attended to. Again, this is a management issue. In one home, for example, the head of the education support service came in regularly to meet with the identified member of staff, to check the details of any new admissions and advise on procedures if there were any exclusions. The head of the unit commented that the member of staff would not have been able to develop the service within the unit without this assistance. An advantage of this external support was that very often the support service had prior knowledge of new admissions, having worked with the child in another context previously – this helped to give some of that continuity which is so slippery in the lives of many young people who are looked-after.

Key workers' responsibilities were clearly laid out where homes had a clear policy. For example, in one, key workers were obliged:

- to meet with the education support service teacher weekly – as needed (the teacher had a fixed time for this weekly visit)

- to visit the child's school at least once every half-term

- to attend educational reviews
- to attend professional network meetings every three months.

In another home in the same authority, a member of staff, completely unprepared insofar as she merely happened to be around and was 'being polite' to the researcher who was waiting to speak with the unit manager, spoke enthusiastically about working with schools, obviously accepting the position as quite the normal, expected thing to do; not insignificantly, she kept saying we do this, we do that – an indication that practice was embedded within the culture of the unit and that it was a team effort, as it were. Previous research has suggested that it often depended on the particular interests of individual key workers as to whether a child's education was promoted.

Partnership with schools

The best of the homes, like the foster carers, worked in partnership with the schools. Establishing relationships with schools was considered one of the most important tasks. This was undertaken in various ways, depending on the confidence and previous experience of the unit manager. In some cases, the unit manager had taken initial responsibility, sometimes with an education support service teacher (who was often 'attached' to the home); once links had been forged, responsibility was delegated to the respective key workers, certainly for day-to-day liaison, although one unit manager said that she always dealt with exclusions 'to show how seriously we take them'. It was interesting to note that when residential care staff spoke of 'an excellent school', and were invited to expand on the criteria they applied to assess excellence, they did not merely identify the fact that the school 'held on the young person at all costs'. Although this may have been a feature, it was related to the principal criterion – that the school collaborated with the residential carers, was open to them and worked with them.

The following is an example of the way in which a residential children's home had identified the specific ways in which this collaboration would be encouraged; the document was to show key workers how they might work to support school placements.

- Arranging a meeting with the head teacher or head of year to:
  - discuss the young person's educational situation
  - set up mutually convenient dates for regular feedback
  - discuss the relevance/necessity for the school to be involved in planning/review meetings
- Keeping school informed of the decisions made at planning meetings/ reviews (should they be unable to attend)
- Informing school of any changes/incidents that might affect the young person's behaviour

- Supporting the school by addressing any problems that may have arisen during the school day
- Supporting the school by discussing with staff and helping to implement behaviour modification programmes – if appropriate
- Attending parents' evening; informing of absences; providing a suitable environment for homework
- Being supportive of the young person and school placement.

The facilitation of this often depended on the way that the link had been set up, the way that communication was managed, and the professional input from the education support service (see chapters two and three). Partners recognised that each had different skills and expertise, and saw different aspects of the young person: together, a change could be effected. A head of a unit pointed out that cause and effect was often very difficult to determine; where perhaps six adults (key worker, support teacher, teachers at school, therapist, unit manager, social worker, for example) were all working intensively with a young person, it was often the combined input which effected a change rather than any one component, particularly where the young person had complex needs and deep-seated difficulties in relating to society.

The input of the education support service

There was evidence that the relationship between the education support service worker attached to a residential home and the staff in that home was a developing one. This was particularly apparent in those authorities which had about five years' experience of this sort of support. In some cases, practice in the residential home was effective before the service got involved; for whatever reason, the carers had always promoted education (the previous NFER research showed that there was good practice in residential homes but it was unsystematic across authorities and a child's chances of meeting it depended on good luck). Elsewhere, once staff within the home had been trained and the culture changed, the support service worker was able to focus on other developmental activities (further details are given in chapter three). Commonly, the support service worker was involved in exclusions, usually because they were thoroughly *au fait* with education law and the statutory position regarding the procedures associated with exclusion. The following comments from unit managers were typical:

'The education support service are invaluable here; the whole thing is a minefield and you can get fobbed off. They know who to approach and what tone to take.'

'I have the courage [to challenge exclusions] but not the jargon.'

Other factors

Purely internally, there was evidence of small touches which helped to 'soften' the institution and make it like a 'normal' home. For example, one unit manager spoke of how staff would ensure that all the young people's equipment for the following day at school was prepared the evening before so that 'there are no hassles in the morning and no excuses for not going'. In another, the unit manager spoke of how she liked the breakfast table to look pretty 'so that they go off feeling good' (the home was noticeable for its 'homely' touches – for example, the children's paintings stuck up in the kitchen and a vase of flowers from the garden on the table). A couple of unit managers said that the young people were taken to school in staff cars – again, to establish 'normality' and to escape the perceived stigma of arriving at school in a minibus labelled 'social services' or the name of the home. These things may appear trivial but there was evidence that they were all part of an ethos which valued school and could be of great significance when the young people concerned were among the most volatile and prone to being upset.

School refusal

All staff interviewed were conscious of the fact that systems needed maintenance and were extremely frail. The point was repeatedly made that there could be 100 per cent attendance one week and then an 'incident' could reduce this significantly. One unit manager, working with extremely disturbed adolescent boys, said attendance could depend on who was on duty or who was in the unit.

All residential staff were accustomed to dealing with school refusers. The following are some examples.

> One manager said: 'It's easy to give up and say "OK don't go to school". But these kids need time to talk things through. Something could have happened at school, or they could have been on the phone to their mum and something upset them. I'll explore why they're not going to school and try to find a solution.'
>
> Another made the same point: 'If someone refuses school you say "why, what's the matter?" and manage the problem – you don't leave it.'
>
> A third told of how school was maintained even if there were other problems – this was part of showing the young person that they were important *qua* person despite how they behaved. One girl absented herself from the home – she was involved in sexual activity in the area; the head of the unit found her in a nearby house at 8 am and took her home: 'I said, "come on, let's get you into school" and she was washed and changed and into school that morning.'

Factors militating against education stability in residential care

All interviewees concurred that the fragility of school attendance was critically influenced by inappropriate admissions: bizarre as it may sound, one new resident could, single-handedly, prevent all previously attending residents from going to school the following morning. A number of anecdotes were told about when this had happened. Sometimes it was because the new resident was a very powerful personality, had no school place on admission, and would not condone others going to school while s/he did not as this would 'look bad' for her/him. In other cases, the new resident might encourage the others to abscond or go off for a night's offending so that they did not go to school the next morning. It was frequently pointed out that many young people with significant difficulties are 'weak' in that they are easily led and quickly succumb to any bullying; thus they are prone to undesirable influences.

Although it is a broad social work issue and outside the direct brief of the present research, the whole issue of emergency admissions is a key one, critical to educational stability in residential care (and relevant, though having, perhaps, less of an impact, in foster homes). Some managers said that admissions were very rarely 'planned', saying that any 'planning' was represented by a telephone call 12, rather than two, hours in advance. Only in one case, a residential home for children under the age of 10, was a three-month lead time referred to. Elsewhere, managers spoke not only of the disruption to routines of having emergency admissions, but also the effect on other residents. It was not just a case of the new resident leading others astray; staff had no time to accustom residents to their new peer, even to tell them about their likes and dislikes. It is, perhaps, easy to forget that even events like these, small though they may seem superficially, create additional stress in the lives of young people who already have so much to cope with. The 'normal' child does not suddenly have to cope with a new person in his or her household; if there is someone, it is usually a positive and happy experience – a friend or relative – not a stranger or someone who may, potentially, be a bully or disrupt a previously harmonious group.

Transforming residential homes

In three notable cases, the unit manager who was interviewed for the NFER research was the person who had 'transformed' the situation in the home. Each had a different tale to tell but each had wrought a sea-change in the ethos and *modus operandi* of the home prior to, or *pari passu* with, transforming the situation *vis-à-vis* education. Although contextual details varied, analysis of the cases suggested that there were characteristics common to each of their approaches. These can be summarised as follows – the order is not significant as contextual variations mean that there were different priorities at different times in the different homes:

- **an acknowledgement of the problem and the design of a strategic plan to address it**
  This strategic plan had the critical theoretical elements of such a plan – i.e. it was not a 'piece of first aid' and managers were aware that changes had to made in a logical order

- **the physical renovation and reorganisation of the home**
  In each case this seemed important – the previous decor and physical organisation did not value the residents or promote an educative approach to problems. The renovation included, for example, reducing the number of beds so that young people could have their own room, creating space where young people and staff could congregate together (staff offices at the backs of buildings, which were, essentially, 'smoking and chatting rooms' were abolished so that staff were obliged to mix with, and thus talk to, the residents); creating opportunities for young people to 'own' the place – photographs on the wall, certificates of achievement displayed in communal areas

- **staff development by involving staff in the management of the home and sharing aims and objectives**
  Interviewees spoke of previous regimes where the manager was someone to be feared, rather than worked with; of ill-defined lines of management; of confused management – e.g. other services using spare space in the home

- **establishing relationships with local schools**
  This was chiefly to assure them that the residential staff would support them in their work with difficult pupils

- **creating active partnerships with the education support service**
  Managers valued colleagues as fellow professionals and entered into negotiations as to roles that each should fulfil; in one authority, this had matured into the establishment of service level agreements between the homes and the service

- **creating routines that supported school attendance**
  This involved such things as establishing quiet places for young people to work; ensuring that if they were not attending school 'they were not having an easy time at home'; collecting useful data and acting on relevant information

- **establishing expectations of staff**
  Managers involved staff in expectations that school was the rightful place for all young people to be

- **making judicious appointments when the opportunity arose**
  One manager commented that she looked for 'the right attitude to education' in candidates who came for interview, admitting that a few years ago she would not have thought about doing this

- **entering into dialogue with senior staff in the authority regarding admissions**
  As the culture changed and became more conducive to education, managers became more uneasy about inappropriate admissions.

Summary

- The research focused on carers recommended as being particularly skilled and experienced at promoting the education of young people for whom they cared; it is unlikely that the majority of looked-after young people enjoy such attention to their education;

- the foster carers promoting education included those with widely different levels of experience of the education system;

- successful practice in residential units depended to a large extent on the quality of leadership of the unit manager; however, in some cases, support teams could enhance residents' education without this leadership;

- in effective residential units, all members of staff were aware of their responsibilities as regards the education of the residents;

- many residential care staff have few qualifications; their ability to enhance the educational experiences of residents is greatly improved where attention is given to their own professional development;

- all carers interviewed were convinced of the importance of education, determined to be advocates for the young people in this respect, keen to work with any available service provision, and prepared to challenge school managers;

- many carers were looking after the most difficult of young people; thus their success was not with 'easy cases' and they gave evidence of dealing with a range of difficulties at school;

- any situation in which a looked-after young person was without a school place had a significantly deleterious effect on his/her care placement, in some cases resulting in its breakdown;

- carers found it extremely stressful when schools regularly rang up to ask them to remove young people from school;

- aware of the necessity to maintain stability in a young person's care placement, social services did, at times, provide support in school to maintain a child there;

- residential care staff agreed that residential units were far harder to manage when residents were not at school and stayed in the unit all day;

- residential care staff were aware of their own inadequacy in trying to provide minimal tuition during school hours for residents without a school place;

- the outreach work of residential care staff was curtailed if they had to remain on-site all day during school hours to look after young people without a school place;

- residential care staff were unanimous in stating that the atmosphere in units was far happier and contented when all residents were secure in school placements;

- all carers greatly valued the practical help and general advice and guidance given by the specialist support service staff;

- carers were generally keen to act in partnership with a range of professionals;

- some residential units had a written education policy with clear aims and supportive practice embedded within the institutional routines, and the responsibility of all staff clearly articulated;

- staff in some residential units went to considerable lengths to stress the value of education and show that school was important;

- an inappropriate admission of a school refuser could immediately disrupt the stable attendance of other residents;

- effective residential children's homes were characterised by: an awareness of the 'problem' of education and the design of a strategic plan to address it, attention to the physical and organisational environment of the unit, a positive attitude towards staff development, the establishment of relations with local schools, active partnership with discrete support services, routines supporting school attendance, high expectations among staff regarding the potential of residents and dialogue with senior managers regarding the appropriateness of admissions.

CHAPTER 6
THE SCHOOLS

This report has considered the work of two of the partners – the education support service and carers; it now focuses on schools and providers of education.

Without exception, all those interviewed believed that the proper place for those young people for whom they were responsible was an ordinary school within the community – by 'ordinary' they meant a school which the child would go to if s/he were not looked-after. Some of the young people discussed by interviewees were, in fact, in special schools (usually for pupils with moderate learning difficulties or emotional and behavioural difficulties): the appropriateness of some of these placements was questioned. In the case study authorities, there was no support for a return to the arrangement whereby young people in residential care attend an education unit attached to the care home: the positive benefits of the 'normality' of a mainstream school, of meeting other adults and young people and of getting away from the tensions which might arise among residents and staff in children's homes, and within foster homes, were universally recognised. Some interviewees who had been involved in education units spoke almost with embarrassment at the level of education which they felt they had provided: the narrowness of the curriculum was thrown into sharp relief by the National Curriculum.

Practitioners did acknowledge, however, that there was a place for alternative courses at key stage four and that it was appropriate for some young people to be engaged on special projects and 'packages' of education, perhaps comprising time at school, college, work experience and a project. They also believed that there might be a case for some off-site provision to be available for young people looked-after who were being reintegrated into school and were not attending full-time. There were cases where such provision had been helpful as a short-term measure. These arrangements will be considered below.

Schools' attitudes to pupils who are looked-after

Carers and education support service workers all said that schools differed enormously as regards their attitudes towards pupils who were looked-after; however, there was no consensus as to whether any particular 'type' of school was more favourably inclined than any other. Some complained about grant maintained schools; but in one authority, the head teacher of a grant maintained school chaired the local area panel addressing the issue of the education of looked-after children. Others found denominational schools helpful while others found that they were more conscious of their 'image'. Elsewhere, the same school shifted its attitude under a new headteacher. 'Best practice' suggested that typecasting schools on the basis of their 'status' was an unproductive exercise. While most education support services had an excellent knowledge of local schools anyway, they were generally of the persuasion that the most creative thing to do was to approach schools and build up a relationship with them so that they were accessible to young people who were looked-after and could be used as a generally available resource where appropriate for a particular young person.

Carers did speak of apparent discrimination from schools, however – although one interviewee suggested that the discrimination was towards the care system rather than towards individual pupils (in practice the difference was probably inconsequential). One foster mother said: 'When you say it's a foster child they think, "Oh ho, here's a problem!", which isn't always the case'. This response was most frequent when schools had had no, or negative, experiences of pupils in the care system. It should be remembered that children who are looked-after represent a tiny minority of the school age population (0.44 per cent), even smaller than the population of pupils with statements of special educational need, and so many schools may go many years without having an application from a child who is looked-after. A member of one of the education support services said: 'The more kids through a school, the better the relations. Further out in the city there's always an air of suspicion'. Another spoke rather wearily of the fact that some schools tended to take up a confrontational position and demand an explanation of why the young person should be admitted – rather than look at strategies to facilitate that admission process:

> 'I approached X high school and they looked at the statement on the boy and said: "This kid's obviously got massive problems. Why should we take him and why do you think he'll be able to fit into mainstream school?". I went through the fact that he had gone through a term at X primary school with no trouble and just had the support of a dinner lady who sat with in the odd lesson to ensure he completed the set work ...'

It is interesting to note that in other circumstances, where they 'like' the young person and find his or her behaviour acceptable, a school will often bend over backwards to persuade the parents to choose that school rather than go to a competitor. Arguably, if schools serve communities, they have responsibilities to *all* those living in them.

The incidents with schools about which carers and support workers chiefly spoke fell into three main categories: admission, exclusion and what might be termed 'general maintenance' – that is, working with the carer to enhance the pupil's prospects.

Admissions

Interviewees commented that one of the most obvious ways in which schools exhibited their prejudice against potential pupils whom they perceived to be 'difficult' was to claim that they had no spare places – in the experience of the carers interviewed, this happened widely. Bearing in mind that looked-after children very often transfer schools at unusual times of the year and term, in some cases it is unsurprising that places were not available. However, both carers and staff from the education support services gave accounts of schools not giving accurate information about available places. One of the functions of the education support services which was regarded highly was that of pursuing the case and eliciting accurate information from the LEA so that carers or social workers (usually with the help of the support service worker) could challenge the school. On numerous occasions pupils had been eventually admitted once the school realised that carers, social workers or other interested individuals were not going to take 'no' for an answer. But what was interesting was the way in which these situations were *managed*, in best practice. Confrontation was avoided if possible – the child was not, after all, going to be advantaged if the school accepted him or her reluctantly (data reported below illustrate how young people can be made to feel unwanted at school).

The position of the school ought, clearly, to be taken into account. Many interviewees spoke of the local interest in league tables and competitiveness among schools: the common perception was that this militated against 'difficult' young people, although it must be said that there was a lack of any hard evidence about this. However, be that as it may, schools nationally are hard-pressed as regards resources and are reluctant to shoulder additional responsibilities without further resources; sometimes the resource issue is indefensible, in that schools may be making decisions to spend money elsewhere, but at others it is justifiable to a certain extent in that schools worry lest they will not be able to meet the pupils' needs with the resources presently available to them. Recent research at the NFER (see Fletcher-Campbell, 1996; Lee *et al.*, 1996) has shown that this had had an impact on the ways in which schools provide for pupils with special educational needs – a case analogous to that of children who are looked-after.

In the light of this scenario, the most important thing is to reassure schools 'that they will not be left alone with the problem', as one interviewee put it. There were various strategies here.

Admission information

A number of those having difficulty seeking entry for a pupil remarked that information about the child, in the form of previous school reports or the pupil's statement, for example, was inaccurate in that it 'was history'. Schools were understandably reluctant to admit a young person who had a poor record when last in school but, as carers and social workers pointed out, that might have been a year ago and a lot of work had been done with him or her in the meantime. A carer said: 'I said [to the school], give him a chance, he's matured since then'. Equally, the poor report might say as much about the previous school as about the pupil. A foster carer remarked:

> 'Sometimes a child comes with a background from another school that hasn't been able to cope. This combines with the fact of their being in care and reflects on the *child*. [The school thinks] "Oh yes, definitely a problem". Sometimes things aren't as bad in a new school.'

Preparation for admissions

The same carer gave the details of the following story.

> Two little boys of primary school age came to her for fostering. The younger one had a statement, for behavioural difficulties, and his older brother had not. Both had a poor record from their previous school but the older boy had picked this up largely because 'he took the can for the little one'. The local primary school refused to take both together. So the carer and social worker got the older one in first, by himself, and support was given by an education support service teacher. He integrated well, was successful, and 'the school saw that he was really nice and praised him and he got a good report'. This success not only made it easier to integrate the younger brother (as the school was less anxious) but the older boy was transferred to another school (when he returned to his natural parents) without any difficulty as he now had a 'good school record'.

In another authority, a teacher from the education support service spoke of how responsibility for admissions should be shared so that schools did not feel that they were taking the blame.

> 'We need to say to schools "this experiment may go wrong – this child has been badly abused" ... In one case we set up all sort of strategies in case things did go wrong – but none was necessary ... but it set everyone's mind at rest.'

The case illustrates how children can greatly benefit from the way in which the case is managed. Another example shows how the management can be taken on by the school itself. The following incident happened at one of the schools recommended to the research team as being skilled in dealing with pupils who are looked-after. It also concerns admission arrangements.

> The school had agreed to offer a place to twin boys who were looked-after and had formidable behaviour difficulties. The special needs co-ordinator spoke of how she had got in touch with the special needs co-ordinator of the boys' previous school in order to discuss their behaviour and learn how colleagues had learnt to manage them at the school. She said that she was aware that the pair were going to present a challenge and that it was necessary to design a strategy prior to their arrival so that the new school was prepared to meet their needs.

This was a real example of positive collaboration between professionals – in this case between two schools. Clearly, the more networks and initiatives of this nature that there are, the more children in need benefit. But the same sort of collaboration arose between other sets of professionals: those initiated by education support service teachers have been described in chapter three. In the following example, the manager and staff of a residential children's home were the initiators; here, they were preparing the school to admit potential pupils who were looked-after.

> A residential children's home changed its focus and became a specialist resource for young children who had been abused. The home backed onto a site on which there were a junior school and an infants school. Initially, the head teacher refused to admit any of the children from the home but, after intervention from the LEA and, more importantly, assurance from the children's home that they would work together in the management of the young people, the head teacher agreed. The relationship developed to the point that the school and home entered into a contract, with the home guaranteeing to support the school with the children's difficulties. They developed joint strategies to reinforce positive behaviour at both home and school. Although there were not children at the school at the time of the interview – the residents happened to be in special schools – the option of school placements there, if appropriate, was available.

> In another example cited, an education support service teacher who had previously worked with a particular difficult child, gave the teachers at the school which was admitting the boy in September support and guidance before term as regards strategies which seemed to be effective in the management of his behaviour. This was, once again, to try to prevent failure and a negative situation arising.

In these examples, it was the teachers who were being prepared. But it may be equally important to prepare *pupils*. There is evidence that this is an important element in peer acceptance of pupils with significant special educational needs and, also, of the victims of bullying. A support teacher gave the following example.

> A young boy was moved to a new primary school at the same time as moving to a residential children's home shortly after horrendous facts about his own natural family had been revealed to him (briefly, to show the enormity of scale, he had mistaken the identity of his natural parents, and had just learnt that his natural father had committed a dire crime). Unsurprisingly in the light of this context, the boy's behaviour was unacceptable. The support teacher and the head teacher of the new school felt that they had to explain to the boy's class what was happening. They spoke with the whole class, telling them that their new peer had a lot of difficulties in his life and sometimes needed to leave the classroom; it was explained to them that this was unusual and there was no excuse for them doing likewise, as they did not have comparable difficulties. The pupils were accepting: as the support teacher said: 'Kids understand this sort of thing time and time again'. The class took on 'ownership' of the boy to the extent that they told the teacher that the boy got on very well with the school nurse and they came up with the suggestion that he should go to the nurse when he was too upset to remain in the classroom.

This was, perhaps, one of the most powerful anecdotes gathered in the course of the research. It was not, in fact, told to the researcher by the interviewee with any degree that it was 'unusual' – this, perhaps, speaks volumes for the support teacher who told it. However, it illustrates inter-agency collaboration (the head teacher and the support teacher), a school determined to be inclusive (by admitting and working with the pupil), the use of any appropriate resource (the school nurse, peer support) and, *pari passu*, the social and moral education of the class involved (seeking their understanding, expecting them to accept a child who might fall victim to bullying/isolation in other circumstances, and involving them in problem-solving).

> In another primary school, two new pupils who were looked-after were admitted in the middle of term. This, clearly, is difficult for any child, as friendships and peer groups have been formed and any new entrant is regarded with suspicion; for children who are looked-after and have recently changed where they live, it is all the more daunting. It was explained to the class that the new pupils might feel lonely (as they were entering mid-term – not because they were looked-after) and that the class were to be kind to them. Kind and thoughtful behaviour was rewarded within the classroom. The two new children settled in well.

Questions can be raised, within the field of moral education, about the acceptability of rewarding kindness (do pupils do it for the reward or because it is kind, for example). Although there may be objections, they are largely irrelevant here – though worthy of discussion elsewhere. The point is that real efforts were made to make the admission *successful* – vitally important for children for whom so much has gone wrong; and, again, the strategy was via the peer group, eliciting inclusive behaviour and support from them.

These stories reiterate the point that once schools have had a 'good experience' of a looked-after young pupil, they will be favourably inclined to other such pupils in the future. This experience strongly reflects that of the integration of pupils with significant special educational needs. Very often, pupils with needs are unwelcome because of the school's fear of the unknown and lack of confidence in coping with something new. Once there has been a successful trail-blazer, as it were, the path for others is cleared. This has important consequences for the whole concept of 'admissions'. Badly managed – that is, 'set up to fail' – they can have disproportionate adverse effects for other young people in the future, as well as providing yet another 'failure' situation for the child concerned. But if they are to be successful, they not only have to be planned, but they have to be planned in collaboration with other carers. Information about admissions and dealings with schools needs to be shared so that these activities can be 'managed' – as seen in chapter three, the specialist education support services were in a prime position to engage personally in the planning process and also to keep oversight of it.

Poor management of admissions

Problems with admissions (and, of course, with exclusion and poor 'maintenance', as described below) could increase the perceptions of the looked-after child that s/he was unwanted. The following case illustrates a number of points.

Sarah was at the point of transferring from primary to secondary school and her foster parents were seeking a suitable placement. Sarah had come into care following a lengthy period of extreme neglect which had caused her to act violently ('she was like a frightened rat') and so had had difficulties in coping with life at her primary school. There was, in fact, a salutary point here in that there had been inadequate preparation for the school and a fully supportive framework had not been established (for which the foster parents had a very high regard in the circumstances – 'some schools give you the brush-off but not this one – a smashing head teacher') as Sarah's care placement was only considered to be short-term. In the event, the foster parents committed themselves to long-term fostering for Sarah. Had this been managed differently, Sarah's primary school experience might have been more positive. Anyway, Sarah was interviewed for a secondary school before the only other applicant from the primary school – a pupil who happened to be the child of a teacher there. The other pupil was offered a place before any notification was sent as regards Sarah; a decision was only sent after the foster parents 'had badgered for one'. They then decided to appeal but there was a long wait and what the foster parents interpreted as delaying tactics – they were given different stories by different members of staff within the authority. Anyway, the upshot was that Sarah was the only member of her year group who did not know where she was going the following term. As the foster mother said: 'this increased her insecurity and feeling of being different'. In the event, following the appeal, there was a meeting at the school for which the foster parents said the headteacher had amassed a number of teachers; the meeting started with the head teacher saying 'we're very wary' and then going through a list of points and demands for which they wanted answers and explanations. The foster parents and the education support service teacher commented: 'We were drained but we set up some positive planning'. The experience would, clearly have been a formidable one for the foster parents – it was set up to be by the head teacher – despite the fact that they were totally committed and determined to get the best for Sarah. In this situation, the presence, support, expertise and experience of the education support service teacher was clearly a critical factor in the ultimate 'success' of the case. The school had, apparently, never thought about setting up some of the more obvious strategies which the support teacher suggested – for example, that Sarah should have a mentor to whom she could turn in difficulties.

This example highlights the fact that, often, what is required to support children who are looked-after would also benefit other young people – as in the case of the mentor. Looked-after children, *qua* group, probably always need this facility – but so do many other young people; this is just a standard element of pastoral care. But if something which really should be there is not in place, the most vulnerable young people suffer disproportionately.

The research reinforced this point over and over again. Of the example presented above, it was remarked that if the school was not prepared to co-operate over the admission of Sarah, it would have undone a lot of the careful and effective work which the foster parents had done with her. This is another critical point. It was frequently observed by those interviewed in the NFER research that all partners had to be aware of 'corporate parenting'; the school here could make or mar work done elsewhere and needed to realise its possibly unique, complementary role. This point also applies to exclusion, as will be discussed below.

In another incident, a couple of foster parents spoke of the disastrous situation when inadequate preparation was made to secure an admission.

> 'We've just had a child who had no educational input. They said that there was a place but wouldn't give us a start date. The kid had just had seven days a week schooling in a secure unit – all his life had been structured ... he came here and there was nothing ... He went haywire.' They told of how difficult it was to occupy him: 'he was frightened of the streets, not bothered about swimming or the pictures ... we used to take him to the shops ... anything to occupy him ... he had no social skills with other kids.'

In this case, the child did not qualify for assistance from the education support service, because of its referral criteria: here, the LEA and youth justice's planning had been inadequate.

Choice of school

The actual school to which admission for a looked-after pupil was sought was often limited by such factors as geographical location (long bus journeys were off-putting to older pupils, younger ones had to be nearer home, some abused children had to be out of the area of their abusers, transport costs were taken into consideration and so forth); previous exclusions (usually relevant only to adolescents) and special needs (if, for example, the child's needs required a special school). The ethos and nature of the school was also taken into account. However, there was evidence that carers, particularly those in the more what might be termed 'educationally mature' environments, where education had been taken seriously for some time, were considering the young person's educational needs and interests. Some carers dismissed some schools as 'having too high academic standards' or 'being too rigid as regards discipline' but others were beginning to think of such things as facilities (for sport, for example) or the opportunity for different, non-GCSE courses leading to alternative accreditation at key stage four. Again, the fact that such criteria, which would be considered in 'normal' circumstances, were being taken seriously by some carers in relation to young people looked-after, was encouraging. Of course, they obviously should be, but there is little previous research evidence to suggest that this is widespread practice. A head of a residential unit said:

> 'We try to divide up the difficult young people among the schools. For a start, we try to match the young people's needs with the school so we are not just dumping them in the nearest school. We look at all the brochures – not just the first available ... Also, it's good that they go to different schools and wear different uniforms and have different friends – it gives them something to talk about when they come in and they don't get involved with other residents' problems at school ... Schools say that they don't mind taking pupils from [this home] because they know that so much thought has gone on beforehand.'

Factors encouraging schools to admit difficult looked-after pupils

By far the most potent factor encouraging schools to admit difficult young people was the guarantee of support – some were, after all, genuinely concerned that they had not the resources to support a young person. One school, which was, in fact, excellent as regards its attitude towards looked-after young people, nevertheless very much welcomed 'just having an extra bod in' because they recognised that 'we cannot give the one-to-one attention that these children need'. A education support service teacher remarked that she was aware that, when contemplating admissions, schools were thinking in terms of what they would be asked for in the future – for example, were support withdrawn or in terms of the pupil's Individual Education Plan.

Exclusions

There is, of course, a considerable corpus of literature on exclusion, much of which is relevant to young people who are looked-after. What follows here will be a discussion of the issues as they pertain particularly to young people who are looked-after and what carers did to ameliorate the situation and try to restore placements following temporary or permanent exclusion. Reference to the effects of exclusions on carers was made in chapter five where the effects on young people were also mentioned. Briefly, the latter include getting out of the routine of going to school; losing touch with the 'normal' social life of school and friends; an increased likelihood of getting involved with a deviant subculture of drugs, crime and offending; exacerbating relationships with carers; and, last but not least, falling behind with school work. As regards the latter, one residential social worker remarked:

'The only thing I don't agree with is when they're actually excluded, our teachers [from the education support service] don't teach them on-site because they say that at home they wouldn't be taught if they were excluded, but my argument is that they're not at home and they are under-achievers anyway, and they're at a disadvantage and they could be at a greater disadvantage being excluded for a week or two weeks and not being educated.'

This is, clearly, a matter for service managers to address but it reinforces the fact that children who are looked-after frequently suffer an accumulation of disadvantages.

Schools' perceived readiness to exclude

It was a widespread perception among those interviewed that many schools more readily excluded pupils who were looked-after than those who were not. Interviewees felt that schools asked carers to remove young people as they knew that, in the case of those in residential care, there would always be someone on duty and, in the case of foster care, that there probably would be someone at home. (As mentioned previously, those fostering the most difficult young people in the research sample rarely had a full-time job elsewhere.) A unit manager made the following observations about an incident in which the school had used what was essentially a minor incident as an excuse to ask the carers to remove the boy:

'At the end of the day, if he was either from a one-parent family who was working, or both parents [were working] ... what would they do? They couldn't phone them up. They wouldn't be sending them home because they have no justified ground to exclude him ... they would have responsibility for that child till ten past three. There is nobody at home so they couldn't send him home. But what did they do. This is a residential unit, 24 hours a day .. they phone us up wanting to send him home ... you know, it's wrong. And with residential units I feel they are too quick to take the easy option. As I say, some schools will work damn hard with us and others will take the easy option.'

It was, thus, easy for the school to dispose of the problem, rather than deal with it using internal resources. There are no hard data about this issue – collecting them would require sensitive ethnographic research methods and the collection of documentation about cases over time. There was no opportunity to question schools about their exclusions within the terms of the NFER research methodology, as the decision had been made only to visit schools which demonstrated positive policies and practice as regards the education of pupils who were looked-after; these schools were, thus, not those accused of excluding inappropriately. But to a certain extent the comparisons are immaterial other than to make a point about justice and that this is another area in which looked-after children face discrimination. The fact remains that exclusion and suspension were frequent occurrences with which carers and education support teachers had to deal and the research sought information about optimal ways for dealing with these incidents.

The schools' position must be recognised. In some cases, schools that tried their utmost with difficult young people nevertheless had to resort to exclusion – particularly for violence to staff or other pupils. And, in many cases, it was necessary for the young people to be excluded as it gave them a message about the boundaries of acceptable and unacceptable behaviour. No social worker or carer interviewed in the course of the research was anything but straightforward and clear that the young people with whom they were dealing had to learn how to fit in society and to control their temper, intransigence or whatever. However, a number of carers questioned whether young people should be 'dumped in exclusion centres' for a particular incident when this incident had been worked through and addressed, and support for the pupil in mainstream was available. Exclusion could be educative but only if the right action followed the event and the incident was effectively managed.

Perceived discrimination against looked-after pupils

There were, however, incidents where, on the evidence presented, it seemed that pupils who were looked-after had been discriminated against. Where two young people were involved in an incident, for example, the looked-after one would be excluded while the other would not. One foster mother presented fairly convincing evidence that her foster daughter's head of year refused to believe anything good of her and would immediately accuse her regardless of the cogency of counter-factual evidence, even from other adults. Although the foster mother acknowledged that the girl could present difficulties, she was rightly angry when the girl was further labelled unjustly. In a group interview, a carer remarked that some schools, having admitted the young person, nevertheless looked for opportunities for exclusion:

> Also they watch looked-after children like hawks for anything that might be going wrong – if they sneeze ... They'll keep records of everything – homework forgotten, chewing gum, a minute late for a lesson ...

In another incident, a school refused the offer of a member of staff at the children's home going in to support the pupil in order to prevent a suspension. Clearly, there may have been issues about the appropriateness of the intervention here; the main grievance was that the matter was not discussed and the opportunity offered for the design of a joint strategy to maintain the pupil's attendance. As one interviewee put it: 'It's OK to lose fairly but not if there's no chance'.

A further anecdote referred to the fact that a head teacher made it plain to the girl concerned that she was unwelcome; this had deeply affected the girl and preyed on her mind. The residential care worker told the story thus (the researcher had just asked if Mary was 'marked out' in the school):

> 'Oh yes! Mary wasn't daft. She knew the situation. The number of meetings we had at that school. I mean, on one occasion and it's [the education support service worker] who was saying to Mary "How are you" and stuff, and the head teacher apparently said to her, and in front of Mary, "Mary is only visiting today, she won't be staying". Now Mary heard this quite clearly, and it's not a kid making it up, she was reiterating this to me over that last two months now, this same statement. She gets it word for word right every time, that she was told, [the educational support service worker] was told that Mary is only visiting, she won't be staying today. And that young person, young people can tend to fabricate the truth, but on this occasion it's an odd thing to make up anyway, and she had reiterated it word for word every now and again when we get talking about different things ... it comes up every time.'

A social services manager remarked that the secondary schools in his area had, officially, a no exclusion policy. However, he thought that this was, in practice, unhelpful: 'It's in name only and the kids are made thoroughly unwelcome at school. And as the exclusion is not formal, the LEA does not have to make alternative arrangements.'

Lack of coherence in behaviour management

Carers mentioned the way in which some schools almost encouraged exclusion by handling pupils unadvisedly. Clearly, the onus is on someone to inform teachers about means of managing difficult young people – examples of education support service staff doing this were given in chapter four. The following account illustrates how disadvantage can accumulate for a child where there is not full communication and collaboration.

'We eventually managed to get him into the local school. He had a lot of problems there, basically because they didn't understand his emotions. The particular time when he was at that school, if you spoke to him in a certain way, he would resent it; and you could say the same thing in a different way and you'd have no reaction. And this is where the staff let him down, because they didn't understand his emotional needs, and he ended up getting excluded from there because if he did anything wrong they said "right, you're not going to do PE" – which he liked. Well, there would be an explosion ... If they said things like "you're not supposed to do that, we'll try this another way", or whatever, they'd have got a better result. They just didn't understand how his mind works. It took me a while to do it but I did, so I knew where the staff had gone wrong. I think that is a problem when you've got a child with emotional needs, if the staff aren't educated ... He didn't know how to cry. If you looked at him you would have thought he was a nasty little boy. He wasn't – he was a little boy hiding behind being a bully. It was an outer shell, so anyone not knowing him would instantly dislike him – inside there was this little child asking for help and it was just knowing how to give it to him. That was the only thing I found with the school – the younger teachers didn't have that know-how. That was part of the reason for being excluded.'

Similar tales were told elsewhere of incidents where school and home were setting different boundaries, thus confusing the child and causing him/her to behave unacceptably. Carers spoke of how it was their perception that schools would give in too readily 'for an easy life'. Although they were extremely sympathetic to the stresses of classroom life and the strain caused in a large class by one extremely difficult child, they nevertheless felt that joint management ought to be discussed as a teacher's action could detract from a lot of hard work in boundary setting done by the carer(s).

Exclusions from out-authority placements

Mention must be made of exclusions which were considered particularly traumatic – those from out-authority residential special schools. There were a number of reports of these. Again, the research did not collect figures about these – it could be that they remained at the forefront of interviewees' minds as they presented such problems. But the perception was that the exclusion, usually without warning, of pupils from what were often extremely expensive out-authority residential special schools ostensibly specialising in young people with complex emotional and behavioural difficulties was the ultimate 'cop-out' and 'passing of the buck'. The fact that these young people were suddenly landed back on the doorstep of their own authority, as it were, having suffered a further failure situation and having, most probably, been previously excluded from all the relevant provision within the authority, caused some officers to despair. It was understandable that some interviewees were intolerant of out-authority residential schools. They made the point that they removed young people from their communities and the very contexts in which many of their social difficulties arose; they returned at the age of 16 with no networks where they were to live and, often, in the words of one officer, 'very little different from what they had been like when they went away five years earlier'. Some thought little (to put it mildly) of what some of these schools had to offer (one foster carer remarked that one of his young people was hopelessly 'over-therapied'); most were disappointed with the results, having naively thought that 'somewhere else will do marvels for these kids for lots of money'.

Inappropriate placements resulting from previous exclusions

These schools were at the sharp edge of the whole issue of the appropriateness of various placements following exclusion from mainstream school or day special school. Again, there is considerable discussion in the special education literature about the efficacy of different therapeutic approaches for young people with emotional and behavioural difficulties, for example. It is not directly relevant to raise these debates here – rather, to examine the particular issues as regards looked-after young people.

Education support service teachers were very often those who were most concerned about inappropriate placements: they had knowledge of different approaches in general terms, the educational and the care needs of the young person concerned and, very often, of the authority's provision. Furthermore, where monitoring out-authority placements for individual children was part of their brief, they often had a working knowledge of other provision used by that authority. One such teacher told of the following incident.

> Discussions were in process regarding a secondary school placement for a girl who had had negative experiences in primary school, largely on account of lack of planning, poor provision pending formal assessment and differences of opinion among professionals as to the optimal provision for her. The girl had recently had two major uproots in her care placement, was on a care order as she was at risk in the community and was having to cope with a new foster family as well as a new primary school. A residential secondary special school for pupils with emotional and behavioural difficulties was recommended by the educational psychologist (who had no intimate knowledge of the care situation). The two possible schools were both some distance away from the girl's new foster home (which was to be long-term). One had only seven girls of

different ages; the other had only three girls. The education support service worker holding the case pointed out that these contexts militated against social integration, which was something that the girl needed extremely urgently in the light of her previous experiences. Placement at either of the schools 'committed her to five years of compounding the system' and negated the work which the foster parents had started 'and so I felt that we must fight'. What really concerned the education service support teacher was that she considered that those recommending the placement had adequate knowledge neither of the personal circumstances of the girl concerned nor of the placements which they were recommending – she did, in fact, suggest that they had not recently visited the schools concerned.

The foster parents, who were interviewed in the NFER research, reinforced what the teacher had said: 'All was done on paperwork ... once they go to EBD school you can't turn them round ... she is making progress on the friendship front now and she deserves to be able to make friendships ... if she'd had no advocate she'd have gone to special school.' Despite the fact that they had no extensive experience of special schools and were not particularly *au fait* with the education system, as it were, they immediately recognised the folly of the suggestion of LEA officers that they should 'try her in special school for six months and then move on to mainstream if all is OK'.

The last comment in the above example has relevance to exclusion and placements for looked-after children generally. There was evidence that schools were sometimes unaware of the lack of confidence with which looked-after pupils approached school. For example, it was the education support service teachers who had to point out that young people would often feel too embarrassed to return to the classroom after an incident. Equally, a school did not realise the problems for young people in actually returning to school after an absence. One said, for example, 'Oh, X is always welcome to return', without any indication that the pupil would need a supportive integration programme to encourage him to return. As the social services officer said: 'As though it's the easiest thing in the world for that boy to return, especially when he'd been behind academically anyway'. Not only will young people be academically uneasy, in that they will have missed work and find it hard to catch up and to understand the current work, but they will also be uneasy socially. During absences, friendships move on, experiences are shared and so on – the absentee can easily be isolated. This problem was often in sharp focus where young people were offered part-time education. For example, one boy was allowed to attend only on Monday mornings and Friday afternoons; although this was 'better than nothing', it was extremely difficult for him both to keep pace with the work and to establish and maintain peer relationships. When the absentee feels isolated from normality anyway, it is not hard to see why positive and proactive support should be put in place to make the classroom a more inviting place.

Well-managed exclusion episodes

Negative exclusion experiences have thus far been described. What, then, were 'well managed' exclusion incidents – ones which did not result in the depressing situation described by a social services team manager? 'Then they're excluded and go into the sidings – the train's gone and there's nowhere else for them to go.'

What marked these out was, to put it platitudinously, an attitude of 'hating the sin but not the sinner'. Schools would exclude for a couple of days, often because they had no option after a violent episode, after which they would invite the pupil in for a meeting with relevant staff, carers and anyone supporting the pupil in school and work out a strategy, and/or contract, for return. Schools actually got on and did something, as it were, rather than arguing about what was or was not the root of the problem (for example, whether the pupil's needs were 'educational' or 'social'). One social services manager said despairingly: 'I said that whatever the cause, this boy *needs help now* to integrate and catch up, having been out of school for so long'. In 'best practice', return to school involved an analysis of the situation and an examination of the support which the young person might need in order to prevent further episodes occurring. Essentially, the procedures were the fundamental management ones of monitoring, review and evaluation.

One unit manager spoke of a case of exclusion where she considered that once the pupil was back in school again, the most important thing to do was to ask questions as to why it had happened in the first place. She was concerned that neither the school nor the home had realised that things were going wrong for the pupil; she felt that if systems were adequate – and this was a context in which both school and home were aware of needs and working co-operatively – then things ought not to have got to exclusion-pitch, as it were. Thus the incident could be used to inform the future management of the case – and, potentially, that of others.

The head of one of the social services education support service believed that exclusion was 'all about working with schools': speed of return was of the essence as was reintegrating the pupil into the school from which they had been excluded – which was much easier than starting afresh with a new school. As regards speed of return, he pointed out that the length of 'processing time' could vary in different area offices. Again, this is something that affects all children but, equally, long delays affect looked-after children disproportionately given the other pressures in their lives and the fact that school placements may be critical to stability in their care placement. The expertise of specialist support teachers in appealing against exclusions – and subsequently working with schools to reintegrate the pupils – was a key factor in positive exclusion management. A number of interviewees considered that it was critical that young people did not become institutionalised at the pupil referral unit and not consider return to mainstream school an option – this is, of course, an issue common to all excluded pupils, not just those who are looked-after.

Some foster parents who had a number of years' experience of fostering and 'took anything that came' had evidence that where the education support service was working with the child, schools were far less ready to exclude – they said that this was largely because the support teachers would take action straightaway and deal with the problem. This particular support service did not work in special schools – demand exceeded supply, priorities had to be set and the feeling was that special schools should have specialist staff with the experience to cope with difficult children. However, the foster parents said: 'If they rear up at [special school] they'll be out in the taxi and out for a week or a month and then permanently'.

A head of a residential unit believed that carers could not sit back and expect schools to be positive without a bit of 'wooing'. She said:

> 'It's essential that you let schools know that you are taking education seriously. In one week I wrote three letters to a head teacher who was going to exclude a girl for non-attendance. We were able to show that she had done school work here at the home when she was non-attending'. She observed that she tried to get empathy with schools and understand their side of the story, 'think what it's like for teachers in schools, get them to think what it's like to be excluded and in care ... schools were excluding because they thought that we'd look after them but we said 'no, we'll work with you to get things going' ... now things are not allowed to get that far'. One of her strategies (also used widely by education support service teachers) was to praise schools for what they were doing with difficult pupils: 'Go to school and congratulate them on the way they're dealing with kids ... You can do things like go to school and say to the head of year, '[the pupil] thinks you're marvellous' – you've then got a friend for that kid.'

Maintenance

The most impressive practice did, clearly, revolve round the prevention of exclusion and positive action to deal with school refusal – this was part of the group of strategies which can be categorised as 'maintenance'. Anyone could participate in this activity. A residential social worker observed:

> 'All of ours manage to maintain it [school] ... and we usually try to pull them out before they're excluded and that's more kind of like with the expertise of the [education support service] staff being able to assess that they need to come out and they can't cope with school at the moment, so for most of the kids here it's successful.'

One education support service has produced a leaflet giving advice on school refusal. This authority collected monthly figures on school refusers in all its children's homes; the point was made that the same residents might not be continually refusing – it might not be a chronic problem. The refusal might be symptomatic of a particularly difficult period in a young person's life or on account of an inappropriate admission to a children's home. Although not condoned, refusal might be short-term and thus tolerable. The leaflet outlined a service approach to refusal problems.

> *Whole home approach*
> - service level agreement with the support service and an education policy in place
> - unified practice within the home
> - good communication between all agencies
> - commitment from all carers to the ethos of school attendance
>
> *Whole school approach*
> - identifying a named link person within the school who has the ability to empathise with the needs of the child
> - all agencies working together
> - flexibility from schools in meeting a child's needs
>
> *Joint approach*
> - effective and regular communication between all agencies in order to reinforce successes and to ensure regular feedback to address failure of plans
> - an identified co-ordinator of education plans
>
> *Addtional elements*
> - a commitment by SSD areas to short-term financial support to offer 'kick start' assistance such as transport, sessional worker
> - a commitment from the LEA for support via home tutor or EWO
> - early intervention by the education support service.

Other initiatives

In the course of the research, carers and support teachers mentioned numerous small, and apparently trivial but nonetheless important, ways in which they worked with schools to enhance the young people's educational experiences. The focus was on prevention rather than crisis management.

Some residential homes had clear expectations of schools. The following is an example of what schools with whom they were working were expected to do for one residential home.

- Identify a named person to liaise with
- Be part of regular feedback meetings with the keyworker in school
- Ensure that the residential home is kept informed of any concerns or difficulties experienced in school
- Attend relevant planning/review meetings
- Supply a copy of the young person's school and homework timetables where appropriate.

Several mentioned the use of 'daybooks' or 'homework' diaries to keep in touch with what the child was doing at school. Some carers spoke wryly of how they tried to keep one step ahead of the young people. One, for example, found that her foster child was telling her that he was not given any homework because he had told the teachers that he was having difficulties at home; while he told the school that he could not do any homework because his foster parents took him out every evening! Another pressed the school to conceive of a system whereby someone could write down her foster child's homework so that she could help him with it; the boy himself found it very difficult to write down what he had to do.

Unsurprisingly, those schools which regarded foster and residential carers as fellow professionals and valued their perspective on the pupil and the additional information which they brought to bear, were much appreciated by carers. Sadly, this positive experience did not seem to be universal. Foster carers spoke of feeling humiliated by head teachers reprimanding them about their foster child and being made to feel 'amateurish'. 'As foster carers we feel that everyone knows better than us. They say, "statistics show ...".'

In one authority it was the perception that schools themselves, knowing that they had the support of carers and support service workers, felt 'safer' and were able 'to take more risks' with the children concerned and try out strategies; this approach then had a knock-on effect on their treatment of other difficult pupils.

Special needs co-ordinators were often instrumental in smoothing the path for looked-after pupils; they were often in possession not only of relevant information but also of the skills which were needed to manage the young people. A foster carer said:

> 'The nice thing about the school is that they've got a good SENCO who's setting up regular reviews and we're getting a lot of information.'

In another school, the special needs co-ordinator regarded writing individual education plans for looked-after pupils as a useful staff development exercise for her colleagues; by getting them to engage in this she was, of course, helping them to understand the particular difficulties of these pupils.

Preparedness to recognise achievement was very important. Although the position here is no different from that of any young person, because looked-after pupils tended to be 'difficult' and to be in trouble at school, it was sometimes hard for teachers 'to see the good side of them'. Some of the authorities which had well-established education support services, held Award Ceremonies, or prize givings, dedicated to recognising the achievements of their looked-after young people; these were extremely motivating events, attended by civic dignitaries, with official guests and so forth (see chapter four for a brief description of one such event). A foster carer was impressed that when the special needs co-ordinator was told that a fostered pupil was going to receive an award she said 'I must go and tell the SMT about that'. A teacher at another school had attended an award ceremony; she admitted to a researcher that 'I struggled to think how this kid could have an award' but had seen him in a new light and had found the occasion an extremely positive experience.

As is often the case, it was sometimes a matter of a young person coming up against the right teacher(s): 'John had a support teacher and also two teachers at his school who were a married couple and had adopted a child of their own and they really did work well with John.'

The overall quality of pastoral care and guidance in a school had a direct impact on the progress of a looked-after pupil's progress at school. As has been pointed out, it is not enough to rest on the fact that these young people are attending – huge though that step and achievement is for many of them; they must be achieving appropriately to their ability, aptitude and interests. Again, the fact is that any slight flaw in the wider context will have a disproportionate effect. In one case, for example, a looked-after adolescent was on the point of exclusion for unacceptable behaviour in school. On the support service teacher's closer examination of the situation, however, it was revealed that the girl had learning difficulties which were neither being understood nor met. It is, after all, unsurprising if any adolescent is 'awkward' if s/he is made to read (in a geography lesson) in front of the whole class if s/he has literacy difficulties; this pupil was behaving inappropriately because the curriculum was inappropriate. The special needs facilities at this school had been neglected and were extremely poor, although the newly appointed special needs co-ordinator championed the girl and was doing the best he could in adverse circumstances. It will be remembered from chapter three that education support service teachers often differentiated curriculum materials for a looked-after pupil – something which, arguably, should be an expectation of any teacher in any classroom, particularly in the light of the Code of Practice and National Curriculum entitlement.

Similarly, some schools were more effective than others as regards supporting pupils to make decisions for option choices – again, this is something which has been found to be critical to the achievement of pupils with learning difficulties at key stage four. One foster mother was aggrieved that her foster daughter had chosen unsuitable options. The school's argument was that they had sent home a parental information sheet. The foster mother's argument was that she had made it clear to the school that the girl should not be given the responsibility of taking important documentation home – she had never received it, in fact.

Alternative education provision

As has been mentioned in chapter two, a number of authorities returned with their questionnaire, details of alternative education provision and projects run either by the authority itself or in collaboration with a voluntary organisation such as Cities in Schools. The present research was not interested in these *per se* – rather, in the opportunities they presented to looked-after young people. Interviewees working with older adolescents were generally very positively disposed to such schemes, particularly when the looked-after young people had been out of school for some time. It was generally considered extremely difficult and, moreover, perhaps inappropriate, to reintegrate pupils back to mainstream school when they were street-wise 15/16 year olds. The alternative projects, usually demanding the routine of the work place, punctuality and engagement in productive work, were considered beneficial. The disadvantages were that they were rarely full-time – so damage could be done if the young person were not usefully occupied for the other hours in the 'school week' – and that places were limited. All interviewees said that they would welcome more provision of this nature.

It ought, perhaps, to be pointed out that it was specific projects that were welcomed. Comments about tuition centres, offering perhaps a few hours a week, were not so generally favourable. Although such centres could be excellent for some young people who did not want to go to school or found it difficult fitting in at school, some carers said that other young people, who wanted to go to mainstream school, found them boring and worthless, recognising that they were being given short change educationally. They could not see the point of going to a centre for perhaps an hour and questioned what, of value, they could learn in an hour. Furthermore, a number of interviewees felt that it was important that alternative projects were run under the auspices of the local education authority. This was for two reasons. First, so that they be part of the education system and that links with mainstream provision were possible and there could 'be somewhere to move on to'. Second, there was the matter of accountability. There was a certain degree of unease about the quality of staffing and work programmes of some schemes which were externally organised.

The flexibility of schools in facilitating negotiated timetables and part-time education as part of packages comprising work experience, college taster course and project work was wholeheartedly welcomed. Very often, unless providers worked together in this way, the young people concerned could not be kept actively occupied for five days a week in school hours.

Initiatives in school clusters

In a couple of the case study authorities, initiatives in clusters of schools were significant. In one, it was observed that the clusters could wield quite a lot of power, particularly if there was the perceived 'threat' of schools opting out and seeking grant maintained status. They would wield significant pooled budgets and be able to make demands of the local education authority – for example, about school places, support and provision – which could be to the benefit of looked-after pupils. For the future, the service might have to consider entering into partnership, or drawing up contracts, with the clusters. There are, again, parallels with practice in special education: there is evidence of considerable benefits to teachers and pupils where schools collaborate over the use and distribution of resources (see, for example, Lunt *et al.*, 1994).

In one area of a case study authority, a cluster of schools had established a multi-disciplinary team to service the cluster. This was in response to the identification, by a member of the education support service, of schools' concerns about communication with the area social services office. These concerns included: phone calls taking a long time to get through or not being returned; meetings being cancelled, starting late, being unduly long; not being invited to meetings and not receiving feedback from them; insufficient time for the completion of review forms; and schools' professional opinions being ignored.

The draft functions of the multi-disciplinary team were as follows.

- To assist schools in the early identification of attendance problems and to develop strategies to bring about an improvement in school attendance;
- to negotiate between school staff, parents and pupils in order to reduce the amount of time at school that children lose as a result of exclusion;
- to advise and assist schools in the preparation of an education plan for children who are looked-after;
- to implement practices and procedures through which children with special educational needs can be assessed with greater speed and efficiency;
- to advise and support schools in making referrals to the social services department in cases where children are in need of protection;
- to assist school staff, pupils and parents with early recognition and management of behaviour which could impede a pupil's progess in school;
- to establish youth work programmes that support and enhance the education they are receiving in school.

A case study of the consequences of 'failure'

Although this report aims to focus on positive practice, the following case study where a school declined to play its part in the equation of support is given in order to show the gravity of the situation. The account was given by a foster mother, who said that it was typical and that she had had similar experiences with young people whom she had previously looked after and had heard similar tales from her fostering colleagues.

John was nearly ten and had been in care for four years. Mrs Smith, his new foster mother, 'picked up John and his younger brother on the Friday, ten days before the start of the Christmas holidays'. He lived about 35 miles from his former placement and so they decided to leave transfer to a new school until January. John had never been excluded from his previous school and his statement entitled him to 21 hours support assistant time; thus Mrs Smith expected the transfer of both him and his brother to be straightforward. 'Then we hit a brick wall.' The local primary school to which she was applying declined to offer an immediate place to John, although it did admit his younger brother; they claimed to have had a bad experience of 'a social services' child' before and asked to see report from his previous school. There were delays while this happened. They then said that the reports were dreadful – though John had never been excluded. Mrs Smith and the social worker pointed out that John had a tremendous amount to cope with when he was at his previous school but was now settling down; furthermore, the school would not have to cope with John with no additional support. As regards this last point, the school said that they would have to advertise, offer and appoint someone to fulfil the role; Mrs Smith realised that this could take months. John very much wanted to go to school.

Meanwhile, Mrs Smith had to keep John at home all day – something that she had not anticipated when she offered the foster placement – apart from a couple of hours a week at a tuition centre which offered tuition to pupils who had no school place. The teachers at the centre suggested that instead of two hours at the centre, they should take John in to the relevant class at the primary school for that time. John still very much wanted to go to school. By this time he had disclosed to his foster carers the abuse to which he had been subjected and, this off his mind and having been reassured that he was not 'a bad boy', was 'completely different'. Why, he asked, was he only allowed to go to school for an hour when the other children were there full-time; 'he was becoming paranoid about himself'. The only 'explanation' that Mrs Smith could give him was that he was being 'punished' for his past behaviour. This was in total contradiction to all the other work that was being done with him to give him a fresh start and say the past was the past.

Meanwhile, the effects on the care situation were significant. John's younger brother taunted him with the fact that he was having fun at school and he had a school place and that John was naughty and so forth to such an extent that his placement broke down as the brothers had to be separated. Although Mrs Smith was able to 'hang on' to John, she spoke of the stress that it put on her in terms of the disrupted day: she had the one child away from 9-3 and had to take John for odd hours. He was extremely bored and became mischievous; he still very much wanted to go to school.

Eventually, after five months of delay and 'much argument', the school relented. However, they refused to allow John to stay at school at lunchtime despite the fact that he presented no problems at school (the support assistance was primarily for his learning difficulties), he was working well, behaving well and 'quite charming'. They said that they were frightened that he might do something. When challenged for evidence that he did constitute a threat, the school were unable to come up with anything other than 'we can see it in his eyes that he is wanting to do something'. The social worker offered to put in an hour's support every day, with someone chosen or approved by the school, in order to supervise John at lunch time; this offer was refused. John, who had had to move schools, family and neighbourhood already, was thus deprived of an important opportunity of socialisation and making friends at lunchtime, was made to feel different and was aware that the past was still hanging round his neck. Eventually, he was allowed to stay for Friday lunchtimes – there was no trouble. John was thrilled and came home full of what he had had for lunch and which friend he had sat next to. He could not, however, understand why he was not allowed to stay every day. He insisted that he 'had tried to be good' and no one had made any complaints about his behaviour. 'Why was he still being made different?' he asked. At the time of the interview, there was still an impasse: John was still only allowed to stay for one lunchtime a week.

This case is unusual in that the child concerned *wanted to go to school*, was, apparently, doing his best to behave appropriately and the school had no empirical evidence of his unacceptable behaviour in that school. In many of the other examples cited by interviewees, not only did the young people not want to go to school but there had been incidents of violence at school which at least gave some justification for a school's reluctance to take them on. As a result of the situation with John's school: the sibling relationship finally broke down, the sibling had to move care placement, the 'hard work' done by both foster carers and John was liable to be reversed, John's positive attitudes towards school and teachers were likely to become negative ones, and different approaches were being taken by significant adults in John's life (the one putting the past behind, the other bringing the past into the present). Although it was not the case, John's care placement could have broken down. Mrs Smith had previously fostered an adolescent who, again, was refused a school place although he very much wanted one. The stresses of having him at home all day meant that the placement had to end so the boy perceived another failure both in terms of care placement and in terms of school.

'Successes'

The criteria for 'success' are discussed in the following chapter. This chapter ends by presenting some examples of 'successes' attributed to schools' work.

A foster mother said:

> 'He's 13 now ... when he was 8 going on 9 he'd kick and fight you and there were no holds barred ... and he's got his act together now. He still has little outbursts. If somebody aggravates him he's not quite able to control his outbursts but those are few and far between – before, it was a regular occurrence. Like I say, it's only the school and the support there that's helped him on. It's the general teaching staff as well. I feel they've given him a chance where other people have said "No", and he's proved that he was worth it. There was talk of him going to a special school because of his behaviour and I said "if you put him in a special school you've lost him", and he's come out a treat. He's a perfectly normal, healthy boy now.'

The following account was given by a residential social worker.

> 'When she first came she was going to a school for learning difficulties ... then she spent time being educated on the premises ... then they decided to give it a go in mainstream and she's done brilliant – more so than anyone could have possibly imagined. She's fitted in really well, she's doing her exams, she's head prefect, head librarian, so she's doing absolutely brilliant. Even the foster parents didn't think she'd succeed, because while she's here she actually kicks off and we get a lot of violence from her. And while she's there she's a totally different person and she's like managed so totally ... because it's something she's really, really wanted. She's always wanted mainstream school because she sees it as ideal to meet friends, meet boyfriends – all those kinds of things. So it's something she's really strived for, and she's just done really, really well, and we wouldn't have been able to do that as a staff group for her ... Well, she isn't going to get great exam results – the teachers aren't expecting that because she's missed out a lot of early years – but her actually just attending, and achieving her self-esteem by going, and being head librarian and head prefect ... She's had to work really hard to get them – they've not just been dished out to her because of her circumstances. So I'd say that in itself is a success.'

An education support service teacher gave this example.

> 'The kid was violent in primary school – he attacked the head teacher with a knife. He was recommended for a special school but I thought "no, he's got potential" and I fought and fought against it. Eventually they reluctantly agreed to let him stay in mainstream school with my support to give him a chance ... Two years later he's still there ... occasionally excluded for a couple of days but generally settled ... He was on a "retainer" at a local special school so that he could transfer quickly with no reassessment if something went wrong but now they feel that things are going so well that he's permanently on the roll at mainstream.'

It only remains to be said: 'Well done them!' In cases like these only part of the success can be attributed to the adults involved – the young person is clearly a key 'partner'.

And a final word ought to go an ordinary, single sex comprehensive school which was doing its best to be inclusive, and devoting a large amount of time to some girls who were looked-after:

> 'We do care about the kids – that they're happy with us here. Kids rise to it – it's good that they've the confidence to talk to us. Sometimes we're best friend, sometimes surrogate parents, sometimes they hate your guts – you just take what they throw at you.'

All importantly, and what they were probably too modest to say, was that they did not throw it back but absorbed it.

Summary

♦　All those involved in the research agreed that the proper place for looked-after children was in 'normal' education – either mainstream or special school – rather than in discrete education units;

♦　it was acknowledged that there was a place for alternative courses at key stage four and that some looked-after young people benefited from special projects and educational packages, provided that these were purposeful and offered full-time, coherent education;

- schools differed considerably in their attitude towards pupils who were looked-after: some were welcoming and supportive while others were extremely wary, believing that all looked-after children represented a difficulty;

- it was often difficult to secure admission to a new school for a pupil who was looked-after;

- schools tended to be frightened by the child's past history rather than look towards a new future for that child;

- admission was more easily secured where cases were well managed, with the school entering into partnership and being offered support and advice, and a strategy to address the pupil's needs being designed well in advance of the pupil's reception;

- there was evidence of effective practice whereby pupils in a receiving class were prepared for the admission, mid-term, of a new (looked-after) peer, thereby easing the situation for the latter;

- the poor management of admissions could severely disadvantage not only the pupil concerned but also other looked-after children who might subsequently seek admission to that school;

- there was some evidence that schools more readily excluded looked-after pupils in the belief that their carers would be available for them at home;

- carers considered that some schools often reacted unreasonably to any slight misdemeanour from a pupil who was looked-after and would exclude or suspend for relatively minor offences;

- in some cases, carers spoke of the inappropriate management of looked-after children at school, often as the result of poor communication of information about the child;

- some young people looked-after were excluded from out-authority residential placements; in some cases, the appropriateness of such placements was severely questioned;

- some schools only excluded looked-after young people with reluctance and of necessity for violent incidents, and managed the return of the young person extremely positively, setting realistic targets and working in partnership with carers and the education support service;

- there was evidence that, to prevent exclusion, the school placements of many looked-after pupils required maintenance, regular monitoring and effective communication;

- some schools had established extremely positive working relations with local children's homes, to the benefit of looked-after children;

- the overall quality of pastoral care and guidance in a school had a significant impact on the progress of looked-after pupils;

- there was evidence of remarkable success with some extremely difficult young people where schools were prepared to support and encourage them and work in collaboration with other agencies.

CHAPTER 7

GENERAL ISSUES, CONCLUSIONS & RECOMMENDATIONS

This chapter will discuss some overarching issues, consider what conclusions can be drawn from the research findings, and offer recommendations emanating from the report.

Resources

As a resource, education support services were overwhelmingly praised and accolades heaped on them by users. Various users said:

> 'They always ask me if we can go to meetings – nothing is ever taken for granted, very polite, the people very, very nice ... they have a firmness but also a gentleness .. they seem to understand the children, probably more than me sometimes .. they're caring and firm.'
>
> 'If they don't succeed then no one else could've done anything else.'
>
> 'The [education support service] keeps them [the children] alive.'
>
> 'They're worth their weight in gold .. even if there were a problem we can sit down and talk to them and they'll explain to you. It's not a case of "sorry we can't help" and the shutters come down. They're always open, ready and very willing to help .... I've nothing but praise for them ... they're a mine of *useful* information.'

Almost without exception, those at the receiving end of service provision wanted 'more of it'. The head teacher of a special school visited remarked of the education support service teacher working at the school: 'He gives the job full hit ... When he doesn't succeed, it's not for want of trying but lack of resources'. However, the services were 'expensive' when regarded as an option or luxury, particularly where there was financial stringency (as was the case nationally at the time of the research). Much seemed to depend on the local political context – both party politics and the inevitable micro-politics of competing resource-users within an authority were apparent here. There were instances when the issue had been adopted by Members across parties and there was all-party support for initiatives to promote the education of looked-after children – as pointed out in chapter two, the Ofsted/SSI report had been a catalyst for action which was often dissociated from political persuasion. Elsewhere, however, it was the perception of some of those interviewed that looked-after young people's chances depended on short-term political fickleness. One reported confusion over reorganisation of residential care in the area, saying that 'the local [political party] want to close all the children's homes to win the next election'. Unfavourable and distorted media coverage could wreak much damage. An area manager in one authority said:

> 'Some say that the work could be done by social workers ... it's down to money and professional jealousies ... it's nothing to do with the work or the rationale of the service ... the question at the moment really is "it's good but can we afford it?" ... there's lots of politics involved.'

Inter-agency collaboration, favoured in theory, became confrontational when decisions had to be made about such things as who paid for transport or a residential place. One foster carer said: 'The department says that the welfare of the child comes first; it does only when the budget can afford it'. The same position applied in schools: some schools cited lack of resources as reasons for excluding or refusing to admit young people whom they perceived as needing additional support (see chapter six). This is a critical issue in special education at present (see Fletcher-Campbell, 1996; Lee *et al.*, 1996). Although there were very often excellent educational and care reasons for not using expensive, out-authority or specialist provision – for example, not removing the child from his/her home community – nevertheless, decisions about placements were made on resource grounds. Interviewees remarked that there were cases where cost-cutting led to a further failure situation for the child – where, for example, adequate support was not provided to maintain a pupil in a mainstream classroom. The result of this was that problems escalated and the situation deteriorated so that more expensive support became critically necessary, both in the school situation and in the care situation. The 'failure' could adversely affect any work that had been done on the care side and, consequently, entail further input of resources there. As one head teacher interviewed remarked: 'Sometimes children have to fail before anyone will pay to sort them out'.

Shortage of resources limited the options open to those making placement decisions. This increased the likelihood of inappropriate placement and, thus, the breakdown of that placement. Dysfunctional placements increased the likelihood of young people presenting adverse behaviour at school. A residential unit manager said: 'There are kids here out of school who would be in school if they were in a different placement'.

A social services manager, despondent about the whole authority approach to fundamental and critical problems, spoke at some length about his perception that arguments about resources meant that children could end up by going down different paths which might radically affect their life chances.

'There's [the EBD special] school but what's the point of sending them there – they get excluded. There's no money for out-authority placements and often schools have difficulty getting extra hours support. If it's behaviour, there is a long time before the statement and one many not be desirable anyway ... [case example cited] .. For older kids, some of the activities on offer in the alternative schemes are more attractive than what's on offer at school ... It's arbitrary where the kids end up. Parents like [special school] because it's less stigma [than care] ... but the education department feels like a different agency and there is no forum to discuss all this. Teenagers in care have frequent moves and we have a bad record of foster breakdowns. Thus [the special school] might be a good thing because it is more stable – parents get relieved of their parenting but their dignity is left in place. But if this route is taken family needs are not addressed ... the special school is referred to as "the divvy school" ... but perhaps we ought to be less squeamish about using them. The alternative is being on the streets. We used to have a CHE – it was awful and I don't approve of it but at least the kids were not on the streets ... The routes taken by individuals are arbitrary ... yes, it's good to have options but not when they're unsystematic. Kids can go to [a residential primary special school] but if life had taken a different turn they might've been permanently removed from their families.'

Here, there are resource problems interacting with issues of uncertain responsibility, assessment and action. The issue parallels that in relation to pupils displaying inappropriate behaviour at school. Sometimes, these young people go down the pastoral care or disciplinary route at school: in secondary schools, they are 'dealt with' by heads of year or pastoral deputies. At others, they go down the special needs route: they are 'dealt with' by special needs co-ordinators, educational psychologists and behaviour or learning support teams. There has been far too little work investigating the longer-term effects of these different, usually arbitrary, responses.

As regards staffing costs, unit managers were aware that if they were to be flexible and be able to respond to requests for support when an incident happened in school, then the unit had to be staffed at a higher level. One unit manager boldly overspent on this score. Another unit spoke of having to appeal to staff's better natures and general motivation if a former resident returned for support and advice. Although no incidents were reported where these returns were specifically related to education – largely because relevant questions were not asked as post-16 work was not specifically part of the research brief – there is adequate evidence elsewhere that domestic problems (such as housing) after leaving care contribute to young people not completing college courses (see for example, Action on Aftercare Consortium, 1996).

Referring to lack of attention to education in a residential unit, a senior officer observed:

> 'It's a struggle just keeping the unit running without trying to involve other agencies ... there are insufficient resources to concentrate on education even though they are well aware of the need for it.'

On a more mundane level, resources to support education could be difficult to secure. A foster carer mentioned that she tried to ensure that teenagers had smart school uniforms – 'they do not like going to school looking tatty' – but that it was sometimes difficult to do this on the allowances she received. A residential carer spoke of the problems providing specialist equipment for school; she cited the example of special art equipment that a student needed for a post-16 course. She had to cater for this sort of thing from a general budget which covered such items as pocket money and personal toiletries. Although she was usually successful in procuring what she wanted for the young people, it entailed much form-filling and caused a delay in producing the items – this, in turn, made the young people feel different and insecure when their peers would probably have it straightaway.

Difficulties in recruiting foster carers have been mentioned earlier in the report and were attributed to lack of resources to encourage carers to take on hard-to-handle adolescents. A social services officer remarked that 'it would be nice if foster carers took on education issues but it might be asking too much of them'. Thus opportunities for enhancing educational opportunities were restricted by fears of losing foster placements. Furthermore, overall shortage of resources meant that there was often little option as regards placements: this led to inappropriate emergency admissions in residential care which, in turn, could disrupt patterns of school attendance which, through a lot of hard work, had been established in that home. Further resources would then have to be directed towards that home in order to repair the situation; these might well be resources which had to be removed from 'less critical' situations.

In terms of access to resources, chiefly it was the most critical cases which attracted the greatest input of additional resources, the exception being one authority where the order of priorities ran children 'in need', children in foster care and children in residential care. The endless debate about the distribution of resources for pupils with special educational needs bears resemblance; here, the basic criterion is that resources should go to the most needy. The salient question is the same: what defines the greatest need? With young people looked-after it is chiefly interpreted as those in crisis. However, those who do not present with problems which are unmanageable in the classroom may be ignored. As a social services manager said: 'I think we sometimes forget that when things are going right, people may also need support'. And a carer said: 'You need regular meetings with schools even when nothing is going wrong'. The whole matter of the under-achievement of looked-after children – something rather different from low-achievement, which is the more easily measurable – has hardly begun to be touched in any systematic way.

Furthermore, there is a parallel issue about the redistribution of resources so that a greater degree of preventative work forestalls the need for crisis interventions. All the specialist education support services involved in the NFER research were aware of the urgency of engaging in such work but were often limited in their ability to do so by resources available, thus setting up a vicious circle. It is, clearly, a senior management responsibility to identify structures for the transfer of resources and to identify where money freed should be targeted. In the present case, it could be for training (by working with) carers, school and natural families.

In summary, the resourcing issues revealed deeper problems associated with the notion of corporate parenting (inter-authority dispute about control of budgets) and long-term and short-term effectiveness. The research literature on the over-representation of those who have been in care within the populations of those without homes and those in custody is unequivocal. One service manager felt that the only way to get through to some policy-makers was to argue the case for educational intervention for looked-after children on economic grounds: they are a vast expense to the tax-payer in later years if appropriate action is not taken. But the cost to *lives* and *people* is far greater: failure accumulating on failure is destructive. The challenge is to put energy and resources into preventative action.

The criteria for success

Interviewees were asked to nominate their criteria for success. Responses varied according to the 'status' of the interviewee – clearly, foster carers had experiences and hopes different from those of social services senior managers. Furthermore, it was pointed out that 'success' was 'limited by resources and circumstances rather than by workers or the service'. In this respect, the broader social environment referred to in chapter one is significant. However, the range of answers reflected respondents' responses to the issue and their conception of what it was possible to achieve. Some examples, showing various degrees of disillusionment and awareness of the *management* of cases, follow.

- 'If they don't scream and shout and run off, I would say that's successful and that very rarely happens.'

- 'What is success for bottom-line kids? No one else can manage them, they have had repeated fostering breakdowns, failed in family centres, committed violent crimes ...'

- 'Well, it's very individual – for example, it could be from a mainstream place without support to getting them out of the house ... Overall, I suppose it's coping better in the community when we've finished with them ... giving them some choice about what to do with the rest of their life ... they've had a rotten childhood and miserable life etc. but you say "get yourself to the point where you can choose". ... Success could be if a kid has been out for many years and they start looking at college courses; or thinking about going into school for a short time.'

- 'What is effective? You must understand and identify effective outcomes.'

- 'Kids often don't do well but that's why social services are involved in the first place – we're dealing with the most troubled, abused, damaged kids around ... there can be a low start base but it's about *progress*.'

Generally, respondents were loathe to identify criteria, preferring instead the notion of appropriateness in context. Furthermore, many respondents spoke of the necessity of valuing any success and not just thinking in terms of academic success. The critical nature of this for lower-achieving pupils has long been recognised (see, for example, Fletcher-Campbell, 1995). A residential care worker spoke of this in relation to one of the young men for whom he was keyworker.

'X is not an education bright young man but he is brilliant with mechanics. He can turn a car inside out, but they will never test him on his ability as a mechanic, will they? What they will do is test him on his ability in science, English, maths ... and find he scores 15 per cent. He feels bad. But if they were to test him on his ability on being a car mechanic he would probably score 80 or 90 per cent ... they are never going to feel good about them[selves] until they have left school and got a job in relation to their identified skills .. He tells me my motorbike inside out. He knows far more about it than I do. But he will never be tested on that. So he is now going to finish his exams feeling crap, get low grades and think "Well, what good am I at anything?" All I ask is why not test him on one extra area ... Yes, I am not saying forget the three Rs and all the basics. Yes, do them, but also if the child has some ability to do well at something, and is seen to do well at some skill which can be deemed as perhaps more on development rather than on education, but which is something they can achieve and they can achieve in an education institution.'

The last clause in this quotation is the most important. All carers strove to reward young people and highlight their positive points; but 'success' in terms of success in enhancing attitudes to, and engagement in, education (and all that implied in terms of raised self-esteem) could not be achieved without a mechanism for exposing the young person's achievement *within the institution of the school*. Thus it was as though the criteria for successful intervention with the young people with whom we are presently concerned could not be achieved without a corporate effort, without a shared commitment to celebration rather than condemnation, to a joint attempt at cracking the fundamental problem as identified in chapter one of this report.

The environment of the social services and education departments

Resources were one of the factors in the external environment which affected the scope of the education support services. The organisation and policy of both the social services and the education departments were others. Where practice seemed to be most effective in terms of attention being given to education by social workers, carers and schools within an area, there was evidence that the issues had been addressed, at least theoretically, on a whole-authority basis; commitment was shown by the Directorate and the relevant assistant directors, as well as those at middle management level. Significant impetus from head of service level (which is where, in the case study authorities – though not necessarily nationally – the change agent was originally located) was supported from above. In such cases, heads of service faced few barriers in gaining access to all relevant committees and were able to put education firmly on the agenda in a whole range of forums. On the available evidence, this tended to be 'happy accident': those involved in the support services spoke of individual education and social service managers either in post or recently in post who had been dedicated to the education of young people looked-after and who cleared the paths, as it were. They also spoke of individual residential unit managers who shared similar ideologies – as was seen in chapter six, this was often because they had an educative, rather than controlling/containing, approach to the care of the young people. In some cases, this coming together of like minds was confined to one area of the authority; in other cases, provision had started from one point and gravitated outwards – usually once word about the provision got around. The challenge then was to rationalise provision and ensure that resources were equitably distributed. Again, these experiences reflect those in special education, where some areas can be well provided for by a particular service and others less so because there has been unsystematic central planning. This model of change, where practice is developed on a small scale in one area, for example, can be effective and there was a school of thought that it provided a sound way forward for other authorities wishing to take action but without significant additional resources to do so.

Not all services enjoyed substantial commitment from Members and senior officers yet, despite this, they thrived on account of their focus on individual case work. The change was bottom-up. There was evidence, however, that there comes a point where policy and practice have to be embedded throughout the authority and in all systems. For this, leadership from senior management is necessary; otherwise service teams could be constantly engaging in small-scale training. Although this was valued – particularly by those on the receiving end – it may not be an entirely effective use of scarce time and resources. An officer in one authority remarked: 'There's a danger of the [education support service] running the show rather than principal social workers doing it automatically'. Coherence could then be a problem: 'everyone doing their thing and no whole plan'. In one authority, a senior officer spoke of 'a gentle and gradual drift' which had had the result that 'education is central in social work adolescent practice – the benefits are obvious'. He said that the debate was over: no one was questioning whether the work was necessary. There was consensus on this: in the case study authorities the motion of the debate was 'who should do this work?' rather than 'should it be done?'.

This represents a watershed, dividing authorities where services are embryonic (see chapter two) and those where they have been born, gone through childhood and adolescence and are now out in the world, as it were. It is, of course, important to remember that there is a third group of authorities – those which presented no evidence of action in this area. The NFER questionnaire data suggested that of the 66 responding authorities, 36 were in this category. As it might be assumed that the authorities which did not respond were not doing anything significant in this area – and that if they were, they would probably have been identified by the research team's networking activities – then the inactive authorities would seem to be approximately three-quarters of all authorities in England and Wales at the time of the research. This estimate may, however, be too pessimistic given that the majority of authorities have adopted the Department of Health's Outcomes materials which include a substantial section on education. It should be pointed out that the questionnaires were administered prior to 1st April 1996 when some of the new unitary authorities started their existence. Clearly, local government reorganisation has affected much social science research latterly.

The future of the services

The watershed between the mature and embryonic authorities was characterised by a recognition that, because of the developmental work that the service had been engaged in and for which teachers were, arguably, required, many relevant people working with young people looked-after had been empowered to promote education. Thus schools were more knowledgeable about their needs, carers had more expertise in liaison with schools, channels of communication all round had been established and procedures had been embedded in management practice at all levels. In these authorities, the vital implementation phase of change had been accomplished and 'embedding' was in process. The fact that practice was embedded meant that some of the work done in awareness raising and establishing procedures was now redundant. As one social services manager said of the education support service: 'They've required us to focus on the consequences of decisions we might take'. The role of the service managers had always been developmental – the services did largely owe their shape, success and direction to the leadership from these people – but in the early stages it was introducing the whole concept of effective education for young people looked-after. After five years or so it was a matter of maintenance and expansion – ensuring that these young people had access to all parts of the education system. In fact, conceptually, the role of the managers on a service level could be perceived as, in the early stages, that of facilitating integration; and, more latterly, of facilitating inclusion. Once again, the model can be likened to that of special education. Fifteen years ago, it was relatively unusual to find a highly qualified, able and experienced special needs co-ordinator in ordinary secondary schools; staff in schools were reliant on access to the specialist learning support services. In the late nineties, it is expected that there will be a member of staff with these qualities in secondary schools, if not in all primary schools. The roles of the support services have, thus, changed.

It would seem unlikely that, whomever the line-manager or paymaster, the role of service manager or, at least, the functions that they perform, will ever be disposable. This is for four main reasons. First, although this report has focused on positive practice in order to show what can be done where there is partnership and inter-agency collaboration, plenty of negative practice was revealed. Research evidence suggested that it was rarely the case that practice was of the best in all geographical areas in the authority, for example: social work teams, residential homes, foster parents all differed considerably in their practice and many had still to be committed to the importance of education in young people's lives.

Second, and related to this, there will always be a significant training need for carers. Not only do both residential and foster carers and social workers come and go (so that there is constant induction needed) but the actual task – what people are trained to do – is affected by the policy context. New paths have to be cut as there are systemic changes. For example, in latter years, services have found that it is more critical to work with schools rather than LEAs, given the relative local power held by each. Local Government Reform, creating smaller unitary authorities which in many cases will have a numerically small population of looked-after children, creates challenges as to how to manage these services. At the time of the research several of the case study authorities were addressing this issue. In one, the newly created authority was committed to continuing the work but the management implications were unclear; in another, the fate of the provision in a newly created authority had yet to be decided.

Third, and to a certain extent occasioned by the second point, all those working effectively with the young people referred to the extreme fragility of the situation on account of the nature of the young people and their families, and the fact that they represented a tiny minority of the total population. With individual children, one adverse incident could retard or reverse all the good work; with groups of children in a 'large' foster placement or residential care, one inappropriate or thoughtless admission could have a similar effect. Life experiences have made many of these children extremely vulnerable, through no fault of their own, and they will continue to need a richer degree of nurturing than many practitioners, accustomed to 'ordinary' children, automatically give. Education support service senior staff spoke frequently of the necessity to keep education on the agenda in some quarters and to keep looked-after children on the agenda in others.

Fourth, there was evidence that the service staff were in a unique position – able to move freely and with professional credibility between social workers and educationalists. They were needed, as one interviewee pointed out, for the very fact that social workers did not have the time to give education high priority. One social services manager spoke despairingly of the way in which, with a limited staff over a wide and 'problem-intensive' area, his team was expected 'to mop up all society's ills'.

How the job is done is another matter. Internally, the managers of established services were reviewing their staffing establishment, particularly as new appointments had to be made. Externally, their plans had to be drawn up in the context of the constant flux of departmental and authority reorganisation. And in their unique case, the services were subject to the vagaries of both education and social services departments, neither of whom was guaranteed to see the work as a *sine qua non* – simply because it is non-statutory, deals with a minority of clients (even for social services) and embraces notions with which senior managers, on account of training and experience, may be unfamiliar.

It is because of all this that it is imperative to look at the differences which the work of the services has made to the lives of children: differences which most 'good' parents would be fighting for relentlessly and unhesitatingly. It is for this reason that the present report has focused on effective practice – practice that yields differences – and successes, while, concomitantly, pointing to what happens when practice is not so well developed.

One of the first people to become unremittingly committed to the practical challenge of improving the education of children looked-after was Tory Laughlan, the founder of the Who Cares? Trust (a voluntary organisation which promotes the needs of young people in the care system and with which many young people looked-after are familiar through its magazine which many local authorities buy for their looked-after children). Tory contributed much to the previous NFER research on the education of children in care. Sadly, she died in 1994. In the first Tory Laughlan Memorial Lecture given at the Royal Society of Arts in June 1995, Sonia Jackson, beginning her lecture, *Transforming Lives: the Crucial Role of Education for Young People in the Care System*, said of Tory:

> 'She wanted a care system that would recognise and celebrate the talents and creativity of young people and open up opportunities for them. She wanted them to aim for success, not just get by.'

and of the *Who Cares?* magazine:

> '[It] doesn't attempt to deny the difficulties that its readers face every day ... but the emphasis is always on how people can overcome those problems and move on.'

There was ample evidence in the NFER research not only that there *are* talents and creativity to be unleashed in the young people but also that, when all are working co-operatively and positively, problems *can* be overcome and young people *can* move on. It is, perhaps, not overstating the case to ask, on the one hand, if we can ignore the moral imperative to ensure that young people are liberated and move on; and, on the other, whether we are comfortable about being responsible – by neglect – for young people remaining static, encumbered by problems caused by the sort of society which all of us of an older generation have to a lesser or greater degree been responsible for shaping. Readers must decide for themselves.

RECOMMENDATIONS

The recommendations which follow are grounded in and assume all those made in the DFE/DoH joint circular and in the Ofsted/SSI report, both of which are essential base documents; there is little point in going over the same ground, even if it is clear that some authorities have not yet taken regard of this guidance. The NFER research endorses all that is recommended in these documents and it is pointed out that what follows makes little sense without this framework. The following points should be regarded as additional, flowing from the empirical research data of the present project. In each case, a conclusion from the research findings is stated and this is then followed by a recommendation.

Commonality

In the 'best practice' authorities, officers worked on a positive model of collaboration and pointed out the similarities in general policy in social services and education – for example, both would probably aim to keep young people within their own community and use out-authority placements as a final resort. Other authorities used a negative model, pointing out the differences between the Children Act 1989 and the Education Act 1988.

In the first instance, the principal aim of departments should be to seek common ground and work from this rather than worry about dichotomies.

Audit of provision

In most authorities there were gaps in provision for young people experiencing significant difficulties at school because of their domestic circumstances – for example, for pupils of a certain age (e.g. no primary school provision), with a particular background (e.g. no support for young people in foster care) or from a particular school (e.g. no support in special schools).

Departments should jointly audit 'alternative' provision (such as pupil referral units, voluntary agency projects, schemes for young offenders, social services' education support), examine admission criteria, identify how provision fits into the education system as a whole and ascertain whether it offers opportunities for integration and inclusion to all the young people for whom the authority has corporate parental responsibility. All those working with young people looked-after should have access to information about the options regarding provision and support.

Awareness of consequences

The research suggested that some schools were unaware that care placements could break down if they refused admission or excluded young people looked-after; and that some social services officers were unaware that inappropriate placements had deleterious effects on the education of looked-after young people.

> *At all levels, practitioners and managers in all areas of social services and education should be aware of the consequences of certain decisions on other areas of the lives of young people looked-after; challenge colleagues taking inappropriate decisions; and take responsibility for the consequences of their own decision-making.*

Flexibility and speed of response

Speed of response is of the essence for young people in care as so many aspects of their lives can deteriorate once there are problems at school. Equally, there was evidence that the input of support must be dictated by current needs rather than allocated on a formula basis with, for example, a fixed amount of time per week per child.

> *Under whatever aegis support services are established, authorities should assume that services are able to be flexible and responsive and that their structure and working procedures allow action to be taken quickly, without undue delay while assessments are made and data collected; management of support time should be close to point of delivery.*

Professional boundaries

In some areas, specialist support services for pupils looked-after were regarded as substitute home tuition or special educational needs support – that is, the services were assuming responsibilities which might more properly have been fulfilled elsewhere.

> *Support services for young people looked-after should have clear roles and responsibilities which in no way overlap with statutory services or other established support services with a wider brief.*

Nature of support

In best practice, support services facilitated integration and inclusion – they were not alternative educators unless responsibilities had been shirked by other colleagues (see above)

> *Support offered by education support services should be intensive (as appropriate) and time-limited by the task identified.*

Partnership

In best practice, successful outcomes were achieved by collaborative, task-related work.

> *In all inputs, the partners should be clearly identified; the partnership should include the young person, the school and the carer(s), together with the social worker and any other professional (for example, therapist, educational psychologist) actively working with the young person at the time. The education support service worker may or may not be part of the partnership, depending on whether s/he is a facilitator or active supporter. The importance of involving natural families should not be forgotten.*

Carers

Positive results were achieved where carers were committed to the importance of education within the young person's care plan.

> *Officers appointing or selecting carers should ensure either that carers are committed to promoting education for young people for whom they are caring and aware of, and able to take, the necessary practical measures; or that they are prepared to undergo some sort of formal or informal training in order to assist them to do this. The training could be 'on-the-job' training by education support service workers.*

Data

Relevant data were being used to monitor, evaluate and reform provision in the most effective practice. Excuses about confidentiality and incompatible systems were being used elsewhere.

> *Inter-departmental groups should address the issue of the production and sharing of data in manageable and useful formats, and should discuss and come to helpful conclusions about issues of confidentiality.*

Service management posts

Heads of education support services were most effective where they had professional credibility within both education and social services departments, and had a high level of management skills.

> *Heads of education support services should be regarded principally as managers and be appointed as much for their management skills as for their experience in both social work and education.*

Support of service management

Heads of education support services had the greatest opportunities to generate effective practice throughout the authority where they were in touch with other managers at all levels within both education and social services departments, and had access to all relevant panels, committees, and decision- and policy-making forums.

> *Senior managers at directorate level should ensure that lines of management are such that heads of education support services have opportunities to participate in all relevant forums and be informed about, and contribute to, all relevant decision-making about related policy and practice.*

REFERENCES

ACTION ON AFTERCARE CONSORTIUM (1996). *Too Much. Too Young. The Failure of Social Policy in Meeting the Needs of Care Leavers.* Ilford: Barnardo's.

ALDGATE, J., HEATH, A., COLTON, M. and SIMON, M. (1993). 'Social work and the education of children in foster care', *Adoption and Fostering*, **17**, 25-34.

AUDIT COMMISSION (1994). *Seen But Not Heard: Co-ordinating Community Child Health and Social Services for Children in Need.* London: HMSO.

BALD, J., BEAN, J. and MEEGAN, F. (1995). *A Book of My Own.* London: Who Cares? Trust.

BIEHAL, N., CLAYDEN, J., STEIN, M. and WADE, J. (1992). *Prepared for Living? A Survey of Young People Leaving the Care of Three Local Authorities.* London: National Children's Bureau.

BIEHAL, N., CLAYDEN, J., STEIN, M. and WADE, J. (1995). *Moving On: Young People and Leaving Care Schemes.* London: HMSO.

BLYTH, E. and MILNER, J. (1994). 'Exclusion from school and victim-blaming', *Oxford Review of Education*, **20**, 3, 293-306.

BROAD, B. (1994). *Leaving Care in the 90s.* London: Royal Philanthropic Society.

CORRICK, H., JONES, D. and WARD, H.(1995). *The Looking After Children Management and Implementation Guide.* London: HMSO.

DARTINGTON SOCIAL RESEARCH UNIT. (1995). *Looking After Children: Assessment and Action Records* (revised version). London: HMSO.

FLETCHER-CAMPBELL, F. (1995). 'Just another piece of paper? Key stage 4 accreditation for pupils with learning difficulties', *British Journal of Special Education*, **23**, 1, 15-18.

FLETCHER-CAMPBELL, F. (1996). *The Resourcing of Special Educational Needs.* Slough: NFER.

FLETCHER-CAMPBELL, F. and HALL, C. (1990). *Changing Schools? Changing People? The Education of Children in Care*. Slough: NFER.

FLETCHER-CAMPBELL, F., HEGARTY, S., MUNN. P., and WELLS, I. (1992). *Integration in the School: Report of UK Case Studies for the OECD/ CERI Project.* Slough: NFER.

GREAT BRITAIN. DEPARTMENT FOR EDUCATION and DEPARTMENT OF HEALTH (1994). *The Education of Children being Looked After by Local Authorities* (Circular Nos 13/94 and DH LAC (94) 11). London: DFE.

GREAT BRITAIN. DEPARTMENT OF HEALTH. SOCIAL SERVICES INSPECTORATE (1994). *Report on the National Survey of Children's Services Plans: Progress Made During 1993*. Birmingham: Social Services Inspectorate.

HOLDSWORTH, N. (1995). 'Excluded children in care "a scandal"', *Times Educ. Suppl.*, **4123**, 7 July, 5.

JACKSON, S. (1987). *The Education of Children in Care*. Bristol: University of Bristol, School of Applied Social Studies.

JACKSON, S. (1988). 'Education and children in care', *Adoption and Fostering*, **12**, 4, 6-10.

JACKSON, S. (1989). 'Residential care and education', *Children and Society*, **2**, 4, 335-50.

JACKSON, S. and KILROE, S. (1995). *The Looking After Children Training Resources Pack.* London: HMSO.

LEE. B. and HENKHUZENS, Z. (1996). *Integration in Progress: Pupils with Special Needs in Mainstream Schools.* Slough: NFER.

LUNT, I., EVANS, J., NORWICH, B. and WEDELL, K. (1994). *Working Together: Inter-school Collaboration for Special Needs.* London: David Fulton.

MEEGAN, F. (1996). 'Corporate parents who fail children in their care', *Times Educ. Suppl.*, **4181,** 16 August, 11.

MENMUIR, R. (1994). 'Involving residential social workers and foster carers in reading with young people in their care: the PRAISE reading project', *Oxford Review of Education*, **20**, 3, 329-38.

McPARLIN, P. (1995). 'We must end this wasteful neglect', *Times Educ. Suppl.*, **4130**, 25 August, 11.

OFFICE FOR STANDARDS IN EDUCATION and GREAT BRITAIN, DEPARTMENT OF HEALTH. SOCIAL SERVICES INSPECTORATE (1995). *The Education of Children who are Looked-After by Local Authorities*. London: Ofsted/SSI.

SEEBOHM REPORT. GREAT BRITAIN. DEPARTMENT OF SOCIAL SERVICES (1968). *Seebohm Report on Local Authority and Allied Social Services*. (Cmnd. 3703). London: HMSO.

STEIN, M. (1994). 'Leaving care, education and career trajectories', *Oxford Review of Education*, **20**, 3, 361-74.

TOPPING, K. and LINDSAY, G. (1992). 'Paired reading: a review of the literature', *Research Papers in Education*, **7**, 3, 199-246.

TRISELIOTIS, J., BORLAND, M., HILL, M. and LAMBERT, L. (1995). *Teenagers and the Social Work Services*. London: HMSO.

UTTING REPORT. GREAT BRITAIN. DEPARTMENT OF HEALTH (1991). *Children in the Public Care: a Review of Residential Care*. London: HMSO.

WARNER REPORT. GREAT BRITAIN. DEPARTMENT OF HEALTH. COMMITTEE OF ENQUIRY INTO THE SELECTION, DEVELOPMENT AND MANAGEMENT OF STAFF IN CHILDREN'S HOMES (1992). *Choosing with Care*. London: HMSO.

WARNOCK REPORT. GREAT BRITAIN. DEPARTMENT of EDUCATION and SCIENCE. COMMITTEE OF ENQUIRY INTO THE EDUCATION OF HANDICAPPED CHILDREN AND YOUNG PEOPLE (1978). *Special Educational Needs* (Cmnd. 7212). London: HMSO.